THE FUTURE WE WANT

THE
FUTURE
WE WANT

RADICAL IDEAS FOR A NEW CENTURY

EDITED BY

**SARAH LEONARD
AND BHASKAR SUNKARA**

METROPOLITAN BOOKS   HENRY HOLT AND COMPANY   NEW YORK

Metropolitan Books
Henry Holt and Company, LLC
Publishers since 1866
175 Fifth Avenue
New York, New York 10010
www.henryholt.com

Metropolitan Books® and [m]® are registered trademarks of
Henry Holt and Company, LLC.

Distributed in Canada by Raincoast Book Distribution Limited

Library of Congress Cataloging-in-Publication data
Names: Leonard, Sarah, (Political scientist) editor. | Sunkara, Bhaskar, editor.
Title: The future we want : radical ideas for a new century / edited by Sarah Leonard
and Bhaskar Sunkara.
Description: First edition. | New York , New York : Metropolitan Books/Henry Holt
and Company, [2016] | Includes bibliographical references.
Identifiers: LCCN 2015021507| ISBN 9780805098297 (trade pbk.) |
ISBN 9780805098303 (e-book)
Subjects: LCSH: Social change—United States. | Political culture—United States. |
United States—Social conditions—21st century.
Classification: LCC HN59.2 .F89 2016 | DDC 306.0973—dc23
LC record available at http://lccn.loc.gov/2015021507

Thanks to *Jacobin* magazine for permission to print adaptations of "The Red and
the Green," "Coda," "Bad Science," "Working for the Weekend," "The Red and the
Black," and "Red Innovation"; to the *Nation* for permission to include "How to Make
Black Lives Really, Truly Matter"; and to the Schomburg Center for Research in Black
Culture for permission to publish a version of "American Policing: Lessons on
Resistance."

Henry Holt books are available for special promotions and premiums.
For details contact: Director, Special Markets.

First Edition 2016

Designed by Kelly S. Too

Printed in the United States of America
10 9 8 7 6 5 4 3 2 1

CONTENTS

THE FUTURE WE WANT

INTRODUCTION

Sarah Leonard

Every election season is a time of bemoaning why millennials won't vote for politicians boldly committed to picking at the edges of their problems. Consider a snapshot of the situation young people face: the unemployment rate for workers under age twenty-five is 18.1 percent; unemployment for black people who have not graduated from high school is 82.5 percent; the people most likely to be shot by police are black twenty-five-to-thirty-four-year-olds; the national student loan debt has surpassed $1 trillion; and the only jobs lucrative enough to pay off college loans are in the financial industry that detonated our economy or Silicon Valley companies deregulating working-class industries.

The future doesn't hold much hope either, with median household income declining 12.4 percent between 2000 and 2011. Having a family is simply harder to afford now. Meanwhile, each new year sets another low record for union density, meaning we have few levers for turning those income numbers around. Unlike most wealthy countries, the United States lacks universal child care and maternity leave, so women are stuck with the same old debates over an impossible work-life balance.

We were told that in the knowledge economy good jobs followed higher education; there are few jobs, and we lock ourselves into miserable ones as quickly as possible to feed the loan sharks. The magazine writers who report on self-indulgent twenty-somethings (think *Time*'s "The Me Me Me Generation" cover), the well-meaning guidance counselors who coach kids to "invest in themselves"—they should save their breath. You don't need a college course to know when you're getting screwed.

The most grotesque feature of the 2016 election is the razor-thin spectrum of solutions proposed by the front runners to a historic set of problems. Lost in the noise of the 2016 election cycle is the fact that no viable candidate offers any hope for a radically more equal society: the policies on offer would merely mitigate the dire inequality that has been growing since Reagan. And this is despite the fact that a majority of Americans express widespread discontent with the country's extreme consolidation of wealth: about three in four Americans think that inequality is a serious problem in the United States. (This places Americans in the mainstream of world opinion, where in all forty-four nations polled by Pew, people think inequality is a big problem facing their countries.) It is this popular dissatisfaction that no doubt accounts for the unexpected surge of support for the unlikely long-shot Democratic candidate, Vermont senator Bernie Sanders, an avowed socialist.

Indeed, the most obvious source of this election's futility is that popular opinion, expressed through elections, has essentially proved to have no influence on policy. According to a now-famous 2014 Princeton and Northwestern study measuring influence in American politics, "economic elites and organized groups representing business interests have substantial independent impacts on U.S. government policy, while mass-based interest groups and average citizens have little or no independent influence." On key issues like gun control, financial reform, and education spending, the policymakers' divergence from popular opinion has been particularly stark.

The United States is now, in effect, an oligarchy. Beyond this sad reckoning lies an even more fundamental problem: there is no better alternative on offer. We need a vision of a better future, one that turns our modern capacity for abundant food, shelter, and health into a guarantee that no one will suffer for their lack.

So when people demand that we vote, you can see why the answer comes back: for what?

The economic crash was not just an ugly fluctuation that we're all trying in good faith to correct. It has provided cover for neoliberal benefit rollbacks—cutting government services in the name of budget crises—in which all of these candidates have participated. Vulnerable people who need the services the most get screwed first: the young, the old, the poor. Eligibility for unemployment benefits has been tightened and opportunities to extend them rejected because we "can't afford them."

A college education is edging beyond reach for many of us. In 2012, Congress restricted Pell grants for low-income college students. While national student debt has surpassed $1 trillion, the federal government has made it impossible to default on these college loans—even your Social Security can be garnished to pay them off. And before students even make it to college, they are subjected to schools with such attenuated budgets that physicians have started prescribing Adderall to poor kids to keep them focused in unruly classrooms whether they have ADD or not. In the words of one doctor, "We've decided as a society that it's too expensive to modify the kid's environment. So we have to modify the kid."

Perhaps it's wise to modify the kid for the brave new world that will await her: one with constantly shifting and disappearing jobs and no safety net of any kind. It is a truism now that no one expects one career. Most people now in college or high school will have six jobs by the time they're twenty-six. And let us not mistake flexible work for fulfilling work. This is an age when the power of the boss is so ascendant over the power of the worker that we can be shuffled around to match precisely the needs of capital. Department stores and retailers now use apps that will inform an employee midway through a workday if their services are no longer needed to match customer demand. About half of early-career hourly workers learn their schedule for the week less than one week in advance. A full day's work, or a "steady" job, is a thing of the past. This is a chronically unstable way to operate in the world, picking up bits of knowledge work, service work, or manual labor as needed.

When asked what factors led to such a dramatic divide between the needs of the average citizen and the actions of the state, Princeton sociologist Martin Gilens, co-author of the 2014 study measuring influence in American politics, cited moneyed lobbying on the one hand, and "the lack of mass organizations that represent and facilitate the voice of ordinary citizens," on the other. "Part of that would be the decline of unions in the country, which has been quite dramatic over the last 30 or 40 years," Gilens added. "And part of it is the lack of a socialist or a worker's party."

It is not only in the United States that unions are crumbling and the safety net is being torched in the name of leaner, more responsible budgets. The Eurozone, which was once touted as the means to a prosperous and peaceful continent, has revealed itself to be nothing more than a continental system of extraction.

Poor countries in southern Europe borrowed money from foreign banks before the devastating financial crisis of 2010, only to find themselves unable to pay them back. To protect the euro, much of this debt was restructured and taken over by the troika—the International Monetary Fund, European Commission, and the European Central Bank—that then forced countries such as Greece, Spain, and Italy to cut social spending to pay off the debts. Now in Greece, for example, unemployment has hit 25 percent in part due to huge public-sector cuts, and infant mortality, suicide, and addiction are all on the rise because the troika has required cuts in health care spending.

For examples of turning radical ideas into platforms for power, we might consider the rise of radical European parties in opposition to this sort of austerity—examples of Gilens' counterweights to oligarchy. As we write, these parties are being buffeted by international creditors and may collapse, but they have far outpaced Americans in organizing militant left institutions. Greece elected Syriza, the first radical leftist, antiausterity party to hold power within the EU. Syriza entered government promising to defy troika mandates and leave debt unpaid rather than starve Greeks. They promised, as well, greater democracy in the workplace, supporting enterprises such as the national television station, which had come under worker control during the crisis. In Spain, the Indignados movement, a sort of precursor to Occupy in the United States, has transformed into a political party called Podemos. They, too, promise to defy EU austerity measures, root out corruption, and devolve more democracy to local councils. These parties are quite different from one another, the former a party born from a fusion of radical-left forces and the other out of a haphazard and less ideologically coherent coalition of regional groups. They will not solve the crisis right away, and may even disintegrate under pressure from the troika, but they provide an example of organizing successfully for power.

The United States has shown glimmers of such radical potential. The surge of youth politicization embodied by Occupy injected class into our public debate back in 2011 and formed connections with antiausterity movements across the world, especially with the Spanish Indignados. More recently, the Black Lives Matter movement for racial justice has forced the whole country to confront not only the violence that oppresses black people in America, but also the recession that black America has suffered since 2001. Parts of the movement are putting forward economic programs.

Like Occupy, Black Lives Matter eschews centralized leadership in favor of a more horizontal structure that privileges local autonomy. On December 13, 2014, some 30,000 people marched through New York City in honor of Michael Brown, Eric Garner, and other black victims of police brutality, creating a new normal in the public's response: today, police shootings, which are no more prevalent than before, regularly make headline news and inspire mass protests. One of President Barack Obama's last acts in office will be limiting military equipment for police departments; his reform barely scratches the surface of the problems with American policing, but is one of the first tangible results of the movement at the federal level. No change would be on the agenda without pressure from the new organization.

Young activists in the United States are embedded in other rising leftist forces as well. Fight for 15 is a low-wage workers' movement that started with promising victories for fast-food workers and has most recently achieved a previously unthinkable $15 minimum wage for all of Los Angeles. The domestic workers' movement, almost entirely run by and representing immigrant women of color, has organized to achieve a domestic workers' bills of rights—which includes the right to overtime, days off, and legal protection from sexual harassment—in New York, California, Massachusetts, and

Hawaii. The debt abolition movement, which emerged from Occupy, has recently been the undoing of Corinthian Colleges, a shady for-profit education company that ripped off thousands of students, a few of whom, in an act of economic disobedience, are now refusing to pay their student debts in protest. The immigrants' rights movement has been tremendously brave, with many young people taking leadership roles and exposing themselves to potential deportation. All of these organizations have enormous challenges ahead of them, especially because most are reliant on centralized labor union and foundation funding and are not self-sustaining through dues or other traditional labor methods. They also represent a tiny fraction of citizens even as they point to creative ways forward.

So where does that leave us? Some across left-of-center American politics have stepped forward to condemn the new activism. If the reaction to Occupy was "what are your demands?"—shorthand for "show us your reasonable think tank–approved white papers"—then the reaction to Black Lives Matter has not been far off. Establishment liberals such as Al Sharpton have condemned the movement for lacking leaders and have demanded a focus on voter registration and mobilization. Black voter registration did surge in Ferguson, Missouri, after Michael Brown's killing by police officer Darren Wilson, but in the poignant words of one activist and scholar, "voting would not have saved Michael Brown." Certainly, voting for Obama has produced little change, either in the treatment of black people by the police and the criminal justice system, or for students and their chronic state of debt, or for the falling incomes of ordinary workers.

The unimaginative stance of established politicos demonstrates a fundamental misunderstanding of grassroots politics. Protests don't write policy in their first months, but rather shift conversations and tell everyone suffering through American capitalism that they are not alone. More important, all of these movements for change ultimately have one focus: on redistribution—of wealth, power, and justice. Their decentralized structures pose challenges, and are sometimes liabilities, but they indicate a real hunger for democracy, one that may manifest itself differently in the future.

In fact, according to a 2011 Pew poll, a higher percentage of Americans between the ages of eighteen and thirty have a more favorable opinion of socialism than of capitalism. This points to a tremendous churn of radical potential, and while we should not get too utopian about its imminent triumph, it is crucial that we, like the rising European parties, articulate the sort of world we would like to see, the world that no leading candidates have promised. This is a world that could only be born with the force of social movements at its back.

It is time, in other words, for ideas big enough to be worthy of the global discontent that put them on the agenda. The ideas in this volume draw on a rich tradition of socialist proposals, long a force in American politics, only recently quashed into obscurity. It's easy to forget that socialist presidential candidate Eugene V. Debs won almost a million votes, twice. Or that hundreds of mayors and local officials were socialists in the first half of the twentieth century, and that Milwaukee elected three "sewer socialist" mayors, the last as late as 1956. Even today, the Senate boasts a self-described democratic socialist, presidential candidate Bernie

Sanders. This is not a strain alien to American soil—despite the neo-McCarthyite language of the Republican Party. The modern GOP accuses every Democrat of being a socialist (we wish!) and slurs progressive taxation, universal health care, and a host of other decent policies as "foreign" and "European" in order to cast suspicion on anyone left of center.

We propose an alternative vision—both reformist and revolutionary, utopian and pragmatic. Leftists have often shied away from suggesting blueprints, thinking them undemocratic. But proposing a course isn't the same thing as imposing one. If the movements we've embraced in the past couple of years are worth taking seriously, it's because they can form the political basis for social plans. People want to know that there is another way.

The openness of young people to socialism may indicate two things: they are fed up with being repeatedly let down by capitalism; and people who came to political consciousness after 1989 do not have a vision of socialism heavily influenced by the Cold War. When the economic crisis hit, there was a resurgence of casual interest in Marx, with headlines like "Why Marxism Is on the Rise Again" and "A Generation of Intellectuals Shaped by 2008 Crash Rescues Marx From History's Dustbin." Some Black Lives Matter activists have taken up the mantle of the Black Panthers, whose vision of socialism confronted centuries of racist exploitation. Newfound engagement resulted from attempts to describe what was happening to us, and Marxism—which describes a system *designed* to produce expropriation at the bottom and growing windfalls at the top—suddenly seemed more convincing than liberal fumbling to explain how Democratic policies generated by people such as former Treasury Secretary Lawrence Summers could have contributed to the disastrous crash.

The socialism we envision, and toward which we take some first steps toward describing in this book, is one that prizes democracy, striving always for the sort of mass redistribution that makes individual human flourishing possible. Our goal is an economic democracy that produces more freedom than we could ever hope for under our current system.

WORKING FOR THE WEEKEND

Chris Maisano

As the US economy entered yet another period of slowdown and unemployment levels in the Eurozone hit record highs, an Internet meme called "Old Economy Steven" started making the rounds. Most memes are frivolous endeavors, devoted to exploiting cats for comedic purposes or projecting feminist fantasies onto Ryan Gosling. But whoever came up with "Old Economy Steven," likely a recent college graduate with mountains of student loan debt and bleak job prospects, was aiming at social critique.

Steven's image looks like a long-forgotten high school yearbook photo of someone's "cool" uncle. With his feathered bangs, wispy mustache, and open-necked collared shirt, Steven seems like the kind of guy who used to spend his Saturday nights cruising the main drag in his Trans Am, scoping babes and blasting Bachman-Turner Overdrive.

Most iterations of the meme contrast the postwar prosperity with the straitened circumstances of today's young workers. Steven pays his yearly tuition at a state college—with his savings from a summer job! He graduates with a liberal arts degree—and actually finds suitable entry-level employment! Eventually he's retiring with five pensions and going on vacation whenever he damn well pleases.

But Steven doesn't just enjoy the material comforts of Old Economy abundance. He possesses a degree of everyday power scarcely imaginable by working people today. Steven can tell his boss to shove it, walk out, and get hired at the factory across the street. If he gets fired at the new job, that's no big deal. He'll just pick up a new one on the way home. If he wants a raise, he can just walk into the boss's office and demand one. Steven may be a working stiff, but he doesn't have to bow before anyone to make ends meet.

Of course, the Old Economy Steven meme is rooted in secondhand nostalgia. Proletarian life has never really been so easy, and not everyone got to taste the fruits of postwar abundance. There's a reason why a dorky-looking white dude named Steven is used as the avatar of working-class security and agency. Still, the message resonates because it speaks to a very real sense of loss, a yearning for a time when the working class, particularly unionized workers, could expect a steadily increasing standard of living and the sense of security and freedom that came with it.

Steven's Old Economy sustained this security for one reason: it was a full-employment economy. A full-employment

vision for the twenty-first century can and must look different from the full-employment realities of the postwar era. Nor
is the call for full employment necessarily bound up with
assumptions about the virtues of work and the vices of
idleness.

We want full employment precisely because it weakens the
disciplinary powers of the boss and opens up possibilities
for less work and more leisure. A full-employment economy
raises the bargaining power and living standards of the working class in the short run and erodes the relative social power
of capital, opening up possibilities for radical social transformation.

By full employment, I mean what most people would
assume it to mean—an economy in which everyone who is
willing and able to work has access to a job. Mainstream economics, however, offers a rather different conception of full
employment, the "Non-Accelerating Inflation Rate of Unemployment." Broadly speaking, NAIRU corresponds to an osten-
sibly "natural" level of unemployment that does not place
significant upward pressure on the rate of inflation. This is
to say, it doesn't reflect the commonsense definition of full
employment at all. It's merely a projection of the number of
unemployed people needed to keep wages and prices down
and maintain investor confidence.

The concept of NAIRU itself is an ideological response to
the political ramifications of the postwar full-employment
economy, where average unemployment levels across the
developed world dipped below 3 percent in the 1960s. This
state of near-full employment dramatically increased working
class leverage by eroding the disciplinary power of the boss,

who could no longer discipline workers by pointing to the unemployed masses outside the factory gates or the office door.

This strengthening of labor's power vis-à-vis capital is reflected in the massive strike wave of the late 1960s and early 1970s, when workers sought not only higher wages and expanded benefits but also a measure of control over the organization and management of the workplace itself. This dramatic shift in the balance of power also played out in innumerable small-scale confrontations between workers and bosses on the shop floor.

In one telling anecdote from the period, an assembly-line worker at GM who skipped work nearly every Monday is confronted by his foreman. When asked why he worked only four days a week, the worker replied, "Because I can't make a living working three days." Who would have the audacity to say that today?

The Polish Marxist economist Michal Kalecki presaged these developments in his classic 1943 essay "Political Aspects of Full Employment." A full-employment economy would, at least in theory, benefit capitalists by boosting the purchasing power of the masses and consequently the profits of companies looking to meet that demand. But as Kalecki observed, capitalist resistance to full-employment policies derives from a different set of concerns.

In a situation of full employment, the power of the boss shrinks not only in the individual workplace but also in the economy as a whole, giving workers a longer leash and raising their capacity to mount a challenge. From capital's point of view, the social and political relations of production that come with it are untenable. Accepting such an economy would be tantamount to unilateral disarmament in the class struggle.

Actual historical experience bears this argument out. The neoliberal order hasn't been very successful in restoring economic growth to postwar-era levels. But it restored elite class power that was threatened politically by a rising tide of worker militancy and the radicalization of important sections of the historical parties of the left.

At just over 8 percent, the US unemployment rate is currently too high to loosen the disciplinary constraints on the working class, and too low to spontaneously generate mass movements of the unemployed for jobs and income. It's up to those of us on the left and in what remains of the labor movement to unite the employed and the unemployed, the organized and the unorganized, the secure and the precarious behind a political program that emphasizes the right to work.

The call for full employment should not be confused with an affirmation of the work ethic at the expense of pleasure and leisure. We agree with Marx's contention that the "true realm of freedom" begins exactly where work ceases and that "the shortening of the working-day is its basic prerequisite." For socialists, freedom is exclusively identified with the time we spend outside the sphere of material production. We find ourselves through the relationships we build with friends, neighbors, and lovers, the political struggles we engage in alongside our comrades, and the creative and artistic endeavors we pursue as ends in themselves.

Until the middle of the twentieth century, even the most conservative sections of the US labor movement embraced the progressive shortening of the working day and the working week as a core of trade unionism. This aspiration united bread-and-butter unionists and revolutionary socialists, the AFL and the IWW, Samuel Gompers and Big Bill Haywood. During the Great Depression, the AFL was instrumental in supporting Alabama senator Hugo Black's effort to pass a thirty-hour workweek bill in Congress. The bill passed the Senate but was opposed by President Franklin Roosevelt, so it had little chance of actually becoming law. It was subsequently watered down and passed as the Fair Labor Standards Act of 1938, which established the forty-hour workweek we know and love today.

After World War II, when the bulk of informed opinion expected the global economy to fall into yet another slump, radicals placed the demand for shorter hours for the same pay near the top of their bargaining agendas. At Ford's colossal River Rouge plant near Detroit, the leftist leaders of UAW Local 660 antagonized both the company and the union's leadership with their demand of "thirty for forty"—thirty hours' work per week for forty hours' pay. UAW militants continued to demand less work for the same pay through the 1970s, when the neoliberal counterrevolution ended those aspirations.

The labor movement had traditionally perceived the demand for full employment and the demand for shorter hours as inextricably linked; progress toward one was simultaneously progress toward the other. Gompers made the case bluntly: "So long as there is one man who seeks employment and cannot obtain it, the hours of labor are too long."

As historians David Roediger and Philip Foner observe in *Our Own Time*, their survey of labor's struggle against the exigencies of capitalist time, the demand for shorter hours sought to address three important goals. First, it tended to unite workers across divides of craft, skill, race, ethnicity, gender, age, and employment status in ways that struggles over wages could not. Second, it compelled the labor movement to take action in the political arena and broaden its appeal beyond its own members. And third, the demand for shorter hours encroached directly on the right of management to organize and control the labor process. If workers could have a say over when to work, what would stop them from eventually demanding control over how to work?

The working day in the United States has not been significantly altered, either through collective bargaining or legislative action, since the passage of the Fair Labor Standards Act in 1938. As the global economy continues its seemingly endless stagnation, it's time to rediscover the lost history of labor's struggle for shorter hours. Unemployment remains stubbornly high while the average annual number of work hours in the United States remains among the highest across the advanced capitalist countries. In 2010, the average US worker spent 1,778 hours on the job. By contrast, workers in many Continental European nations and the Scandinavian social democracies enjoy a much larger amount of leisure time, and at higher rates of labor market participation. To a significant extent, they have averted the social disaster of mass unemployment through work-sharing schemes and other policies aimed at preventing workers from falling into long-term joblessness.

Scores of studies have demonstrated that unemployment and weak attachments to the labor force are deeply damaging to the physical and emotional well-being of those who experience them. Ending their plight should be among the main short-term goals of the left quite apart from any larger strategic agenda we may advance. So long as we remain within the coordinates of a capitalist political economy, the only thing worse than having a job is not having one. And as the experience of the social democracies has shown, it's possible to maintain high rates of employment, shorter working times, and robust welfare states—even in a neoliberal era.

At the end of *The General Theory of Employment, Interest, and Money*, John Maynard Keynes surveyed the dire political-economic scene of the mid-1930s and summed it up in a single, incisive phrase: "The outstanding faults of the economic society in which we live are its failure to provide for full employment and its arbitrary and inequitable distribution of wealth and incomes."

After the long detour of the postwar Golden Era, those thirty glorious years in which the advanced capitalist countries appeared to square the circle of economic growth and social welfare, we find ourselves once again in the same predicament. Then as now, the program is clear: tax the rich, put people to work, shorten hours, and build the welfare state. These are the demands on which a coalition of left-liberals, social democrats, and radicals might build while appealing to a broad and deeply insecure public. The current situation calls for nothing less.

Considering the paralysis and dysfunction of our political system, the seemingly impregnable dominance of our economic elites, and the drastic erosion in the size and strength of our labor movement, it seems hopelessly utopian to raise the demand for full employment. But it's precisely the utopianism of the demand that makes it so compelling—and necessary—today.

The call for shorter working hours and full employment is the sort of transitional demand that has the possibility of not only appealing to the very real and immediate needs of millions. It also raises the possibility of shifting the balance of power between workers and capital and laying the groundwork for more radical and permanent changes in the basic structure of the political economy. It constitutes a central component of the strategy that should guide the theory and practice of a revitalized left.

IMAGINING SOCIALIST EDUCATION

Megan Erickson

In a large studio flooded with light, young children dance barefoot around a life-size paper tree adorned with white cutout snowflakes. In another classroom, thirteen six-year-olds are seated crisscross-applesauce in a circle underneath red hanging lanterns and a Chinese dragon, listening politely to their teacher.

Down the hall, in a laboratory, middle-school kids dissect frogs and crawfish, using an iPad to record their work. During art class, the children sprawl out in a circle surrounded by couches and hardwood floors instead of desks. The computer lab hosts classes in videography, engineering, and 3-D printing. The rooftop is a playground. This is not the education of the future—or at least not everyone's future.

This is Avenues: The World School, a private for-profit that opened in the fall of 2011 on New York City's Upper West Side, with plans to expand to China, India, Latin America, Africa, the Middle East, the Pacific rim, and Europe in the coming years, with the idea that students can transfer seamlessly from one campus to another. At Avenues, teachers commonly have decades of experience, and turnover is low. Students begin immersion in a second language as preschoolers. Student government assemblies convene twice every six days. Discussion is the preferred pedagogy.

Echoing the leftist writer Paul Goodman's vision of the city itself as a replacement for the institution of school, Avenues informs prospective families that Broadway, Wall Street, the Museum of Modern Art, and the United Nations are its "classrooms waiting to happen." The reality seems to live up to the hype: in 2013, the *New York Times* described a field trip taken by a group of four-year-olds, not to the local park or post office or pizza shop, but to a gallery to view the abstractions of artist John A. Parks, who records childhood memories in finger paint. The same week, older children had listened to a presentation by Sam Talbot from *Top Chef.*

In the frenzied fever dream of American free-market capitalism, everything is for sale, including education. Tuition at Avenues exceeds $45,000 annually, more—but only just—than at prestigious Horace Mann ($44,405), Trinity ($43,320), Ethical Culture ($43,265), Spence ($43,135), and Dalton ($41,350).[1] For the sake of comparison: the median household income in New York City is a bracing $50,711 annually. Wealthy families choose these places not merely as an indicator of status, which they have in spades, but also because unlike today's public schools, a private education offers a wide-ranging liberal arts curriculum in which art, music, and athletics feature equally alongside reading, writing, and arithmetic. And they are willing to pay dearly for the privilege, forking over the equivalent of the down payment for a house *each year* of attendance, from pre-K to twelfth grade.[2]

What does it mean to want "the best education money can buy" (as the *Times* has called Avenues) for your child? What does it mean to get it? What is being bought and what is being sold?

At Avenues there are cognac leather lounge chairs in the library instead of the standard-issue maroon and navy metal stacking ones, and sushi is served for lunch instead of curdled chocolate milk and cheese product. On a fall tour of another New York City private school I attended, families were offered wine and cheese and candlelight while listening to high school students give enthusiastic presentations on how the school had prepared them for meaningful and fulfilling lives. (Not jobs. Not careers. *Lives*.) A sign-up sheet for parent-teacher conferences outside of one of the classrooms had been water-colored by hand.[3]

But the value of such an education is not merely a matter of details: beyond aesthetics, what is most striking about the expensive and usually progressive learning environments favored by rich, well-connected parents—dubbed "the Montessori Mafia" by the *Wall Street Journal*—is how divorced they are from the mathematics of competition. The systematic evaluation, comparison, schedule-tinkering, and budget-cutting to which public-school teachers and children—the labor force of tomorrow—are subjected on a daily basis in

America are nowhere to be found in the schools of the elite. More than anything, captains of industry seem to want a decommodified learning experience for their children.[4]

The educational philosophy at AltSchool, for example, the profitable tech venture founded by a former Google executive, with funding from Mark Zuckerberg and locations in Palo Alto, San Francisco, and Brooklyn, is student-centered learning[5]—there are no report cards or bells rung at the end of class. Students forge their own paths of study. (Tuition is $20,875.)

Thousands of dollars a year buys an interdisciplinary curriculum founded on inquiry-based learning, dramatically smaller class sizes than those in public schools, and early immersion in a second or third language. It buys respect for the voices of students, which is written into Avenues' staff recruiting documents. It buys respect for the students' powerful parents, who have a say in everything that goes on inside, down to the food that is served. It buys an intangible but omnipresent assumption of community competence, of teachers and students. These children are given the freedom to be seen holistically, to be appreciated for their agency, to develop self-possession and actualization—they have the luxury of time to grow. In fact, these thousands of dollars buy an approximation of an education based on equality, a socialist education, without redistribution for the 1 percent.

Only about five million of America's fifty million school-age children, or 10 percent, attend private schools each year.[6] The cultural significance of private schools has never been in numbers, but in the reasons why parents choose to shelter or segregate their child from the "common" schools. In the early twentieth century, the question of whether parochial schools should receive state funding divided Congress. In the 1950s and '60s, southerners enrolled their children in "country day schools"—the original schools of choice—to avoid court-ordered desegregation.

Today's private-school parents appear to be seeking an education that cultivates "fully developed human beings fit for a variety of labors, ready to face any change of production, and to whom the different social functions he performs, are but so many modes of giving free scope to his own natural and acquired powers." The vision is from Karl Marx, but the person envisaged is the trumpeted knowledge workers of the twenty-first century—creative, flexible, assertive, inventive, comfortable in diverse contexts—that American CEOs so vocally demand, and the kind of human beings that schools like Avenues are built to foster.

And yet the real demand for such knowledge workers or for members of what Richard Florida calls "the creative class" is low. According to the US Bureau of Labor Statistics, the information sector is projected to see decreases in relevant employment from 2012 to 2022. On the other hand, health care support occupations are projected to grow 28.1 percent in that period; health care practitioners and technicians, 21.5 percent; personal care and service occupations, 20.9 percent; and construction and extraction, 21 percent. Of these occupations, only those for health care practitioners and technicians fit Florida's definition of the "creative professional" subset of the creative class, and none is part of the "super creative core" of engineers, computer programmers, educators, and arts, design, and media workers. Two-thirds of the thirty occupations with the largest projected employment increase in the next decade will not require postsecondary education. The jobs of the future will be overwhelmingly in the service sector, with little call for those inventive, flexible, and fully developed workers.

Perhaps this explains why the philosophy of education at a school like Avenues, or at Sidwell Friends—a highly selective and progressive private school chosen by President Barack Obama for his daughters whose alumni include Al Gore III, Chelsea Clinton, and Davis Guggenheim, director of *Waiting for Superman*—is so starkly different from the punitive approach at public and charter schools such as the KIPP chain, embraced and prescribed for the masses by neoliberal education reformers, including Secretary of Education Arne Duncan.

Compare the Avenues experience to the feeling of a child walking into many public schools for the first time in the same city, through hallways lined with surveillance cameras and garbage, into a roach-infested classroom with peeling paint and windows nailed shut. The cafeteria and toilets are dirty. Classes for "disruptive students" are sometimes held in trailers.

A survey carried out by the New York City Healthy Schools Working Group, in which schools self-reported on learning environments, found all of these things in a significant percentage of schools: for example, almost half of New York City public schools have bathrooms that lack soap and toilet paper, for example, just under a third have visible roach or rat infestations, and 24 percent have inadequate heating.

And then there are metal detectors, self-evidently unnecessary in private schools, but used in 9 percent of American high schools and 3 percent of elementary schools, despite the fact that no conclusive evidence exists that they prevent violence inside or outside of schools, where most child homicides occur. Several studies have actually found that metal detector programs are associated with lower student perceptions of safety.

In New York City, a national leader in developing school-based surveillance programs, eighty-four public schools have permanent metal detectors in place, meaning approximately ninety-nine thousand of the city's one million students enter their school the way adults enter security checkpoints at airports or court buildings. Since 2002, the city has spent more than $221 million on police and security equipment, compared to $100 million on textbooks and $9.2 million on iPads. And in 2006, then mayor Michael Bloomberg announced the "roving metal detector" program, which gave the New York Police Department the power to conduct random searches of all the city's secondary schools. Cops have seized cell phones, iPods, food, and school supplies from students during searches. Multiple students have been detained for refusing to be scanned.

Negotiating the pressures and humiliations of such an environment demands an intense level of emotional resilience daily from adolescents. When in 2007 City University of New York sociologist Jen Weiss asked kids at New York City public high schools how they thought security staff perceived them, they responded with the following adjectives: *up to no good, hoodlums, felonists, delinquents, loud troublemakers, criminals, deviants, either selling drugs or wannabe future rappers, wearing baggy jeans and hoodies, or short skirts if you're a girl.* One African-American male student told Weiss, "If you look like a description, if you look suspicious, you'll be confronted most of the time."

"They treat us like criminals, not children," a Norman Thomas High School student named Julia told the ACLU in a report from the same year. (In 2010 only 55 percent of students at Norman Thomas graduated on time; a year later, Norman Thomas was closed due to poor performance and turned into three smaller schools.)

In the first minutes of my first day teaching a tenth-grade all-boys civics class on community organizing at the Urban Assembly Academy of Government in Law in Chinatown—where 82 percent of children qualify for free lunch, 91 percent are black or Latino, and in one year, there was a nearly 50 percent teacher turnover rate—an administrator ran into the classroom and shouted at a group of tenth-grade boys, "Who did it?" One of the boys pointed at another. "He did." Without questioning, the administrator angrily escorted the boy out of the classroom. Only then did I begin my prepared lesson on student protests during the civil rights movement.

When I asked students at Urban Assembly to talk about what they liked or did not like about the world around them, they brought up the repressive environment in which they spent the most hours of the day and the unfairness of the principal, who was universally despised. At first I tried to get them to think bigger, to talk about the world outside the school walls. Then I realized that in fact they were thinking big, and we started talking about the power dynamics of the school and its grotesquely undemocratic system of discipline.

At the end of the semester, one child thanked me for

putting up with them. I wonder what effect this kind of schooling has on the life of a child, when students from low-income families are essentially told that they ought to be muted, grateful, and full of "grit," when they walk to class through metal detectors, symbols of imprisonment and freshly averted danger, and are routinely assessed like objects in a factory, based on answers they bubble in on a Scantron test.

Meanwhile, middle-class children learn the gospel of perseverance. As economic stratification intensifies, it is increasingly necessary for even the comfortably off to prove that they've worked to earn their place in the socioeconomic hierarchy. This is the reason for the recent proliferation of the harmful "standards and accountability" movement. While children in urban schools in low-income districts spend twice the amount of time preparing for standardized tests as students in suburban districts,[7] the career-oriented pedagogy of constant evaluation and pressure has taken hold of middle-class schools as well.

If the purpose of schooling is to shape children into productive adults, then school administrators are right to fear them. Children are by definition inefficient and resistant to discipline. Play, the "work of the child," in Vivian Gussin Paley's words, is, in the logic of capitalism, wasted time. When we think about school as a place where children are molded into productive adults, the need for constant observation in the form of surveillance cameras and constant evaluation in the form of standardized tests becomes apparent. Metal detectors are an effective way of communicating to untrustworthy children that they are being watched, and high-stakes assessments are a way of weeding out the good from the bad.

School occupies a complicated ideological space in public life. Throughout its history, the American education system has been assigned a multitude of conflicting conceptual tasks by parents, educators, community leaders, and politicians: promoting "racial uplift," enabling upper-class white women to "save" working-class children with moral education, furthering ethnic assimilation, segregating children of color and poor children, institutionalizing integration, redressing historical injustices, sorting and preparing children for their adult roles, and functioning as a de facto social safety net.

The current role, which involves turning out measurable, productive graduates from the system, has its ideological roots (most recently) in the breathess 1983 report, *A Nation at Risk: The Imperative for Educational Reform*.

The "risk" of *A Nation at Risk* was that high schools were not preparing kids to compete in a global economy. America's schools were falling behind, and so too would its "prosperity, security, and civility." The language of the report is as vague as it is urgent, conflating the perceived failures of the public schools with a threat to national security with no evidence, support, or even acknowledgment that this was a contentious supposition in the first place. An often-repeated—and entirely unsubstantiated—line argues that "the educational foundations of our society are presently being eroded by a rising tide of mediocrity that threatens our very existence as a people. What was unimaginable a generation ago has begun to occur—others are matching and surpassing our educational attainments."

A list of action items to be implemented immediately to save the problem included: performance-based salaries for teachers, the use of standardized tests for evaluation, grade placement determined by progress rather than by age, the shuttling of disruptive students to alternative schools, increased homework load, attendance policies with incentives and sanctions, and the extension of the school day—in other words, longer, harder hours. Each of these solutions was rooted in the logic of free enterprise, taken straight from the playbooks of corporate managers. As I've written elsewhere, the role of public schools had been reimagined as a kind of baptism by fire into the competitive world of adulthood.

The report was and continues to be a seminal document for key players in the current American education policy regime. Mirroring the insistence in *A Nation at Risk* that "We must demand the best effort and performance of all students, whether they are gifted or less able, affluent or disadvantaged, whether destined for college, the farm, or industry," contemporary education reformers have refocused their efforts from equalizing inputs—resources from books to desks to teachers' salaries—to a broad call for higher expectations or outputs for *all* students, regardless of socioeconomic status.

The movement toward higher standards and market-based reforms ignited by the report took place within the historical context of an intensifying stratification of resources along race and class lines and the division of people into leaders and subordinates. The leaders are now overwhelmingly adult administrators, philanthropists, and venture capitalists (usually men), while the people who are most affected by education reform are teachers (usually women) and children with comparatively little or no economic power. The business leader and

the education reformer seek to improve the measurable outcomes of schools because childhood, in the logic of capitalism, is a temporary setback from productivity that must
be overcome.

Since the political transition marked by *A Nation at Risk*,
an accelerating national obsession with productivity and free-
market solutions has influenced the way schools are assessed
and funded to an unprecedented degree: rather than focusing
on equality of inputs (student-to-teacher ratio, teacher salaries,
the variation of funds from district to district), schools are
measured based on equality of outputs—ensuring that every
student produces the same results. But invariably, interventions that are applied to "all children" come to benefit privileged children most.

The crisis now faced in schools is one of inequality and
wealth distribution. Schools are financed through an idiosyn-
cratic combination of local, state, and federal funds, with 83
cents of every dollar spent on education coming from state
budgets and local wealth via property taxes. (The Constitu-
tion implicitly reserves power over public education for state
and local governments, and local control of the schools has
been fiercely upheld throughout the nation's history, particularly by conservatives.) High-income districts—and high-
income schools within those districts—end up with more
money to spend on education than their less wealthy counterparts, and unlike in most other OECD countries, federal
funding does little to equalize resources among rich and poor
students.

Yet one of the most robust and consistent findings of
education researchers is that social class significantly impacts

educational outcomes from early childhood through college.[8] Studies have found that economic stress and financial constraints negatively affected academic outcomes. Merely identifying as lower or working class is associated with feelings of not belonging and an intention to drop out among college students. Today, over 20 percent of children in the United States live in poverty, and more than one million students in America were homeless during the 2010–2011 school year. At the same time, the nation has seen a long-term rise in housing segregation by income and accelerating resegregation of the public schools that corresponds to the general rise in income inequality since the 1980s, with 28 percent of lower-income households located in a majority lower-income census tract and 18 percent of high-income households located in a majority upper-income tract as of 2010. Researchers have found that intense racial and economic segregation is linked to negative educational conditions and outcomes.[9] As the income gap grows in the United States and globally, so too does the achievement gap between high-income and low-income students.

The project of neoliberal business "reformers" of education is to replace student-centered, play-based, or inquiry-based learning with skill-based academics in public schools because they lend themselves to measurable tasks and outcomes and re-create a specific power dynamic between teacher and learner. Measurable outcomes ideally should lead to an ability to assess whether all children are being given an equitable education, which will in theory lead to a more equal society. But, as the radical educator and scholar Jean Anyon writes, "Family income consistently predicts children's academic and cognitive performance, even when other family characteristics are taken into account"—meaning the effects of poverty on health and well-being outweigh other factors. As of 2002:

> The two best-scoring entities in the United States were the Naperville, Illinois, Public School District and the self-proclaimed "First-in-the-World" Consortium (composed of school districts from the Chicago North Shore area). Both of these entities have high levels of funding and serve low numbers of impoverished students, and both earned high achievement scores comparable to those of Hong Kong, Japan, and other top-scoring countries. In contrast, the two worst-scoring U.S. entities were the Miami-Dade County Public Schools in Florida and the Rochester School District in New York. Both of these receive low levels of funding and serve many poor students, and each earned low achievement scores similar to those of the worst-scoring nations in the study—Turkey, Jordan, and Iran.[10]

In a capitalist economy, schools by their nature as institutions embedded in the social structure cultivate and reward different characteristics in students from different class backgrounds. Marxist economists Samuel Bowles and Herbert Gintis (1976), and more recently, Anyon have written detailed accounts of the political economy of education, explicating how the social hierarchies of school systems correspond to the social relations of the economic superstructure.

It should therefore come as no surprise that despite reformist rhetoric about educating "all children," American public schools work far better for some children than for others by design. The overwhelming mythology upon which free-market society is based is meritocracy—the idea that school is where the best children will succeed and others fail, the same way that companies do. In practice, public school teachers become managers and children become increasingly efficient laborers, or failures. Children who go to schools like Avenues are given a ticket out of this system altogether.

The fact is that education can function as an instrument of oppression or of liberation, sometimes simultaneously. Under capitalism, schools are both a form of social control and a site of community organization and mobilization. Significantly, as Anyon points out, "Rising education levels have often been associated with rebellion against social strictures."

Indeed, there are signs of mobilization around resistance to standardized testing. In the fall of 2014, more than five thousand twelfth-graders in Colorado staged a mass walkout from new state tests in science and social studies designed by Pearson, the largest corporate creator of educational testing materials and textbooks. In a video released the week of the protest, students argued that the tests put undue pressure on them even as they prepared college applications and took SATs. They objected to the fact that the law mandating the tests was passed "with few public hearings, and more importantly, no student input." They point out that funding for education that year had dropped by 6 percent, and that the $36 million spent on the test could have paid the salary of thousands of teachers or paid for the revamping of technological infrastructure.[11]

Then in March 2015, an estimated one thousand students

walked out of school on the first day of testing for a new state standardized test, the Partnership for Assessment of Readiness for College and Careers (PARCC) test, another Pearson-designed Common Core-standards-aligned test used in eleven states. In New Mexico, it is a requirement for graduation. Students from neighboring schools joined together to protest: "The test is taking away students' opportunities to learn in their optimal state and it's taking away teachers' opportunity to teach how they teach best," high school junior Daniel Schilling told the local news channel, WKBN 27. "Our teachers always tell us, 'use our voices,' so why not use it here?" said Gwen Prior, a high-school student. "We hope the governor hears us and does something about this," Julie Guevara, sixteen, told the *Guardian*. "We're not going away and plan to do this again until the testing is done." Demonstrations lasted for a week.[12]

In April, every single eleventh-grader at Nathan Hale High School in Seattle opted out of a state standardized test after their teachers came out against the tests' alignment to Common Core standards.[13] The same month, more than 175,000 students in New York opted out of Common Core English Language Arts exams, according to the New York State Allies for Public Education, an enormous increase from 60,000 to 70,000 the year before. That spring, Florida, Maine, Pennsylvania, and Michigan also saw mass optouts.[14]

There are two possible responses to state coercion through public institutions. Leftists can withdraw from the institution or they can critique it, overtake it, and rebuild it. Anarchists such as Paul Goodman, who believed in burning down public

schools, tend to advocate the former. Socialists must embrace
the latter.

Taking a handful of kids out of the system, whether that
means educating them in expensive private schools such as
Avenues or "unschooling," does not make education more
democratic—it makes it fair and enjoyable for a select few who
have the resources to share in these possibilities. Exceptional,
student-centered learning environments for the financial and
intellectual elite can only ever be an imitation of a democratic
education, since they will always be class-segregated, even in
a society with a far more equal distribution of wealth than the
United States has at present.

They teach upper-class children self-confidence and self-
respect—values that are freeing and democratic when prac-
ticed among all children, but that, when purchased for and
bestowed on individual children, are nothing more than competitive weapons, enabling those who have them to succeed in
a job interview, for example. A video produced by Sweden's
main labor union, the TCO, satirizes the effect of socialism for
a few by depicting a man who "lives like a Swede" in isolation:
enjoying six months of paternity leave at 90 percent pay, hiring
a personal trainer through a government stipend, vacationing
for six to eight weeks a year. His friend explains, "Why does
Joe live like a Swede? Because he can. Working for his dad and
being rich give him opportunities other mortals can't afford."

Visions for education that do not involve a socialist capture
of the state apparatus to ameliorate the vast material inequal-
ities of our society will only be that: a simulation of a socialist education. And there's no path to capturing state power
besides a sweeping redistribution of resources. Changing the

style and substance of the experience inside schools is impossible without changing the material inequities outside them.

A truly "public" school system in which every child receives an *equal* and *democratic* education (which does not mean the same education for all) would, however, be revolutionary. Marx and Engels were ambiguous about what socialist education would look like, since "circumstances are changed by men and the educator himself must be educated," but the contradictions of capitalism can serve as a starting point for the construction of pragmatic solutions, however contingent, that will transform institutions.

In the past, "freedom schools" have come in a variety of forms. SNCC schools organized by Septima Clark, Ella Baker, and other black women educators and used to build critical consciousness in the Jim Crow South invented a pedagogy in line with Paulo Freire's, in which teacher and student are both regarded as subjects capable of action.

The Black Panther Party experimented with a single school based in Oakland, California, that emphasized academic skill development over doctrine, as well as a more widespread series of liberation schools that indoctrinated students in BPP values using a style similar to the "banking model" of education Freire decried, where children were seen as receptacles for the knowledge of the teacher/authority figure. The constant thread in each of these efforts was a focus on collective work over competition.

The importance of public education is its immense and radical possibility as a collective undertaking toward what Freire called "the problem of humanization," in which every single human being has a stake. Whatever form it takes, education

HOW TO MAKE BLACK LIVES REALLY, TRULY MATTER

Jesse A. Myerson and Mychal Denzel Smith

The year 2015 found the United States in the midst of a movement to upend white supremacy. Thousands of people across the country, acting in response to the unpunished killings of Trayvon Martin, Jordan Davis, Rekia Boyd, Eric Garner, Renisha McBride, Michael Brown, and so many more unarmed black people who have lost their lives to police or vigilante violence, took to the streets to proclaim that "black lives matter." A powerful proclamation all its own, it deserves to be strengthened by a vision of what it will take to make those lives really matter in America.

In 1966, along with A. Philip Randolph, Bayard Rustin, and other organizers and scholars, Martin Luther King Jr. released the now all-but-forgotten Freedom Budget for All Americans, which included full employment, universal health care, and good housing for all. "The Freedom Budget is essential if the Negro people are to make further progress," King wrote. "It is essential if we are to maintain social peace. It is a political necessity." King came to espouse this view toward the end of his life, acknowledging that civil and voting rights were a critical but merely a partial victory in the struggle for complete equality.

King's vision, needless to say, was never realized. This is why we propose that, in addition to calls for police reform, it is vital for the defeat of the racist system that the Black Lives Matter movement advance an economic program. We cannot undo racism in America without confronting our country's history of economically exploiting black Americans. Demands from Ferguson Action and other groups have included full employment, and this foundational item is one that can and should be fleshed out, as we hope to do here.

Before laying out our proposals, we should clarify why, historically, eliminating racism requires an economic program. America's story is one of economic exploitation, driving the creation and maintenance of racism over time. The inception of our country's economic system condemned black people to an underclass for a practical rather than bigoted reason: the exploitation of African labor. Imported Africans were prevented by customs and language barriers from entering into contracts, and unlike the indigenous population, their lack of familiarity with the terrain prevented them from running away from their slavers. To morally justify an economy dependent on oppression, in a nation newly founded on the rights of men to freedom, it was necessary to socially construct a biological fiction called race, one that deemed some people subhuman, mere property. "During the revolutionary era," Karen E. Fields and Barbara J. Fields write in their book *Racecraft: The Soul of Inequality in American Life*, "people who favored slavery and people who opposed it collaborated in identifying the racial incapacity of Afro-Americans as the explanation for enslavement." White citizens, making their fortunes and proving their social standing through the ownership of African persons, codified the idea of race into law. Those of African origin would come to form the lowest class of American life, while people of West European origin were free to extract labor and wealth from their bodies. Material inequality, in other words, preceded the racist rationale.

This didn't change with Emancipation. The convict-leasing system, the lynching of black business owners, and the razing of economically independent black towns by white citizens' councils and the Ku Klux Klan made it impossible for the former slaves to flourish. After Reconstruction, the ideology of race that erected Jim Crow society was crucial for maintaining class divisions among whites. As the Fieldses write, "One group of white people outranked the other precisely because it was in a position to oppress and exploit black people." Thus, through the daily experience of this dynamic, "the creed of white supremacy" was bolstered, in the words of historian C. Vann Woodward, "in the bosom of a white man working for a black man's wages."

As a result, black Americans continued to experience racist violence, both physical and economic, and no corrective policy prescriptions were forthcoming. In his book *The Condemnation of Blackness*, Khalil Gibran Muhammad, director of the Schomburg Center for Research in Black Culture, notes that the progressive movements of the late nineteenth and early twentieth centuries advocated increased government resources for poor immigrant groups while continuing to attribute black poverty to the alleged cultural and moral deficiencies of African Americans. This legacy haunts us today in every new injunction that ending racism depends on young black people wearing belts. And it lives in the widespread rejection of the obvious fact that drug abuse, violence, and educational failure don't breed poverty; poverty breeds *them*. The large-scale relegation of black Americans to poverty is the essential "race" problem.

In the postwar boom, as Ta-Nehisi Coates details in his article for *The Atlantic*, "The Case for Reparations," black people were largely locked out of home ownership, the largest driver of the wealth gap in modern America, and further housing discrimination meant that black people were also not allowed to attend the schools offering the highest-quality education—another factor in gaining well-paid jobs. The "New Jim Crow" of mass incarceration via the "war on drugs" has replaced vagrancy laws and convict leasing, but with similar results: robbing large numbers of black people of economic opportunities while also denying them access to federal programs aimed at alleviating poverty. A person with a felony record is denied access to food stamps, welfare, and public housing. And with no wealth to speak of in a country where political participation is predicated on dollars and cents, black Americans continue to lack political representation; the repercussions include an absence of choice in who is speaking for them in Congress and in which mayor or police chief has jurisdiction over their neighborhood. Inadequate economic security is literally a life-and-death matter for black Americans.

It is vital for the defeat of racism that the Black Lives Matter movement shut down the economic engines propelling the continuous reinforcement of white supremacy. Only through the redress of black America's economic grievances (the pronounced disparities in terms of income, wealth, and community resources such as housing, health care, and education) can we begin building a just society.

TRUE FULL EMPLOYMENT

Nothing would do more to transform the current political economy than what is at the core of the Freedom Budget and mentioned in the Ferguson Action demands: a policy of full employment.

What we mean by that phrase—an "involuntary unemployment rate" of 0 percent—differs from what mainstream economists mean, even those who nominally support it. By "full employment" they usually mean *nearly* full employment. During the most recent period of "full employment" (the also dubiously named "Clinton economic boom"), the unemployment rate never dipped below 3.8 percent. However powerful the boom, millions of people in certain corners of the economy were relegated to a permanent state of bust. The people deepest in those corners, the least employed people in the United States, are teenage black high school dropouts from poor families, on whom is currently imposed the conscience-rattling unemployment rate of 95 percent.

It is clear that we require more than the conventional

policies for boosting job growth if we are to meet the demand
for full employment. Luckily, there are two policies up to the
task: a federally funded job guarantee and a universal basic
income that is unattached to employment. By offering employment as a guaranteed right, the federal government could
direct capital to the communities where it is most desperately
needed, while employing those communities themselves to do
the work needed to improve their own quality of life: cleaning and replacing those oft-decried broken windows, filling
potholes, caring for the children of working parents and for
the elderly, clearing slum housing and replacing it with decent
housing. By paying a basic living wage and normal benefits
for a federal employee, the program would effectively set a
minimum wage and standard of treatment for private-sector
employment. In boom times, when there is danger of inflation,
the program and its budget would automatically shrink, and
during downturns, when inflation is extremely unlikely, it
would grow to fill the gap.

This program could and should be paired with a universal
basic income, which King called "the simplest . . . and most
effective" approach to eliminating poverty, citing three essential virtues of the program. First, poor people, their consumption directly subsidized, will no longer want for basic
comforts. Second, the political position of the marginalized
would grow stronger: "Negroes," King wrote, "will have a
greater effect on discrimination when they have the additional
weapon of cash to use in their struggle." Finally, King highlighted the "host of positive psychological changes" that universal material security would yield: "The dignity of the
individual will flourish when the decisions concerning his life

are in his own hands. . . . Personal conflicts between husband, wife, and children will diminish when the unjust measurement of human worth on a scale of dollars is eliminated." This psychological relaxation is the direct negation of the anxiety and terror that persistently accompany black American life.

A twofold full-employment program would mightily advance the fight against mass incarceration and racist policing. Guaranteeing access to employment and income would also reduce prison recidivism. Employing people to handle "broken windows" would transform the trappings of poverty from an excuse for police harassment to paid community work. And millions of people whose livelihoods are currently dependent on an ever-expanding prison-industrial complex would be able to secure employment and income elsewhere, allowing stronger working-class organizing for a rollback of the prison state. Currently, prison closures have devastating effects on the communities for which these institutions act as economic anchors.

A TAX OVERHAUL

In the current economy, we tax labor and industry, which suppresses employment and offshore profit, and we leave the real-estate sector mostly untaxed, encouraging the accumulation of real-estate fortunes. Real-estate property includes not just buildings but, crucially, the land upon which they're situated. The buildings themselves—such as plumbing and woodwork—deteriorate over time until they require refurbishing, so the speculative commodity in real estate, the investment that stands a chance of appreciating in value over time, is really just land. Speculation in the land market has instituted a great deal of the structural racism that characterizes white supremacy today.

The postwar impetus to maintain segregationist housing policies was the protection of property value. When millions of southern-born blacks swept into northern cities, millions of whites fled for new suburban residential developments, taking their capital with them and driving down the land value in black areas. White home buyers (who make up the vast majority of home buyers nationally), with their wealth bound up in real estate, wouldn't have black people depreciating it with their proximity. Moreover, the Federal Housing Administration, in a policy designed to protect this access to landed wealth, was more likely to guarantee mortgages in communities that adopted racially exclusive charters. This policy "redlined" neighborhoods with low "residential security," or land value, depriving black neighborhoods of access to financial services for decades.

The appreciation of land value was at the heart of Wall Street's recent mortgage bubble and its racist predatory lending, by which 53 percent of all black wealth was destroyed. "Mortgage investors," meaning land-market speculators, would buy up houses and sell them once the land value had increased, making off with the gain. To keep prices rising, the real-estate/financial complex offloaded garbage loans on unsuspecting black families, who have suffered a massive wave of foreclosures in the years since the crash.

Education is also linked to land value. Pegging school resources to property taxes undermines equality from two directions: well-to-do people are driven to move into ever more expensive neighborhoods for fear that their kids will be conscripted into inferior schools (thereby further concentrating education funding), while schools in poor areas degrade as wealth flees, driving down land value in the already underserved area.

Keeping land untaxed also gives landowners an incentive not to develop properties in poor areas, since it's thereby free to hang on to an undeveloped plot until white people decide that the neighborhood is "up-and-coming" and bid up the land value. In the short term, this leads to abandoned buildings and vacant lots—that is, to slums plagued with "broken windows." In the long term, it has a catastrophic effect on communities: while these plots of land remain undeveloped, our tax system holds down the housing supply at a time when a severe urban housing shortage has city land prices skyrocketing. And this, in turn, fuels a community-bulldozing wave of gentrification whose primary beneficiaries are the land-speculating interests.

To stop those interests, we must shift from taxing labor and move toward taxing monopoly and land rents. The American political economist Henry George, whom King cited in his economic advocacy, famously proposed a 100 percent land-value tax as the only tax capable of ensuring equality amid economic development. As the board game Monopoly (invented by George devotees) makes clear, even when everyone starts with equal money, private rent extraction inevitably directs all funds into a few hands. George saw taxing the full rental value of land as the only way to develop an economy equitably—that is to say, without producing poverty constantly. And several local jurisdictions in George's native

Pennsylvania do tax land, albeit not at 100 percent. No human created the land, and so no one—not an absentee slumlord, not Goldman Sachs—should be extracting its value from the people who live on it.

BABY BONDS

In the end, black people in poor areas will always be vulnerable to disastrous community disruption as long as white people control the vast majority of wealth. It is wealth (the stock of overall resources someone controls) rather than income (the inflow someone receives over a year) that ensures true economic security—waiving the income a job provides is less intimidating to a person with independent wealth. As bad as income inequality is in the United States, wealth inequality is even worse, as those born rich get richer and those born poor stay that way. As long as white people can take advantage of lopsided bargaining positions to outbid black people for land use, the land remains whites' to claim and distribute. The only true and permanent way to alleviate the many ills detailed here is to close the racial wealth gap.

The political challenges to implementing a reparations program—which we support—were daunting from the outset and are now possibly prohibitive. To address this dilemma, Duke University's William A. Darity Jr. and the New School's Darrick Hamilton have proposed another innovative program that they estimate would close the wealth gap within a few generations. Even those who cannot concede our premise—that black people have been condemned to poverty by public policy, not by their own lack of ambition and discipline—will surely agree that no newborn child is to blame for his or her impoverished condition, and that each one deserves a fair chance at leading a fulfilling and comfortable life. Darity and Hamilton have thus suggested a "baby bond" program aimed at these newborns. Everyone born into a "wealth-poor" family (any family below the median net-wealth position) would be granted a trust fund at birth that would mature when the person reaches eighteen years, whereupon the grantee would obtain access to the fund. The farther below median the family is, the larger the fund the infant would receive, such that the lowest quartile would receive a $50,000 or $60,000 bond. Note that although this program is not limited to the descendants of black slaves, its effect is quite similar to the one desired from a reparations program: eliminating the wealth advantage that white Americans command over their black countrymen.

Karen E. Fields and Barbara J. Fields highlight law professor Derrick Bell's 1990 essay "After We're Gone: Prudent Speculations on America in a Post-Racial Epoch," in which the writer imagines space aliens purchasing all the black people from the United States, whereupon "post-racial America" must truly confront, "straightforwardly, for the first time . . . the problem of who gets what part of the nation's wealth, and why." With white supremacy gone as an organizing principle for social relations, it becomes clear that resource distribution was the question all along. Implementing a program of guaranteed employment and income, a taxation policy targeting monopoly and land rents, and a system of wealth-equalizing baby

SEX CLASS

Sarah Leonard

Pop feminism in the twenty-first century has developed as a series of false choices between work and family, pleasure and duty. The most insidious is this: there is a "work-life balance" that, when struck, will allow a woman to "have it all." It's no revelation that the ubiquitous incitement to *have* everything is code for *doing* everything—the privilege to change diapers and make spreadsheets. And while women seek a balance between two loads that are too heavy in any proportion, the debate typically focuses on white collar lives, eliding the fact that 70 percent of families are not caring for their children alone, but rather with the help of domestic workers and other child care providers. The women who are lauded for "doing it all" usually have help. The women who help usually don't. And working-class women have always "done it all."

What we find reflected in this uneasy divide between women who work inside and outside the home is the struggle that women have always faced under capitalism: they are required to engage in both production and reproduction.

Popular magazine articles and Oprah-style television shows falsely represent work-life balance as an individual challenge, a lifestyle choice available to all women. The feminism on offer is woefully thin and unpleasurable. On the high end of the income scale, feminism seems to mean working even more than men. The media celebrate women such as Yahoo CEO Marissa Mayer and former secretary of state and presidential candidate Hillary Clinton for their brutal work ethics—magazine articles report, awestruck, that they barely sleep, that their staffs struggle to match their work hours, that they've become the rare female leaders in their spheres by laboring harder than male colleagues. Mayer reported proudly that while at Google, she would sleep under her desk.

By this measure, feminism, that utopian striving for equality that we've carried through centuries of opposition, is boiled down merely to the right to work ourselves to death. If feminism means the right to sleep under my desk, then screw it. And this is a vision that can be palatable, just barely, only at the high end of the economy where work is plausibly couched in self-actualization.

Poorer women are left out of the popular conversation entirely because there's no way to paint a veneer of fulfillment on low-income hard work and long hours cleaning houses, working cash registers, and caring for other people's children. This is wage labor, and nothing but. Specifically, women represent about 95 percent of domestic workers,

93 percent of nurses, and 76 percent of teachers, and on average make 78 cents on the male dollar. They occupy the underpaid caring professions and dominate the underground care economy.

Single mothers are penalized, meanwhile, by the structure of welfare laws and government policy. Everything from insurance to your housing options becomes more difficult and more expensive as a single parent.

By every measure, up and down the income scale, women are unequal. And every day we're fed stories of exceptions that, upon closer scrutiny, prove the rule. Women still work a double day—wage and kitchen—and they get paid less for the part of their work that is actually compensated.

What women are grappling with, whether they're rich or poor, is the relationship between care work and wage work. Magazines' encouragement that women (but never men) "have it all" carries the implicit assumption that women continue to be primary caregivers no matter what they do outside the home. Everything for them is described deceptively as a choice. The women who care for those women's children have to balance that work with care for their own children, often residing in the nanny's country of origin while their mother works in a wealthy country such as the United States. Their work frequently goes unrecognized as "real" work specifically because it is the sort of work that is women's "natural" lot. This has made it particularly difficult for domestic workers to organize; many employers (including legislators) don't want anything so transactional as employment law infiltrating their haven. So employers call their nanny "part of the family." They premise the relationship on a language of love and nature and care instead of work. Meanwhile, only half of full-time nannies enjoy paid personal days and only half report receiving paid national and religious holidays. The self-confidence of the woman who works outside the home rests on the exploitation of women working within it.

But even this framework fails to take account of the global chains implicated in wealthy care practices. Domestic and nanny work are being imported from the global South like never before. Migration itself has been feminized due to the demand for care work, and motherly love has become a precious commodity pursued by mostly white women who find it in the global circuits of labor carrying women of color from their own families to foreign homes where they hope to make enough money to support their kids. Women in wealthier countries, increasingly following the same career pattern as men, find that they still need someone to be the housewife— in New York alone, there are nearly half a million children under thirteen with two working parents. As more women in the global North enter the waged labor force, more women in the global South migrate to perform care labor. The "doing it all" narrative falls utterly by the wayside: these women have no household to return to at night. And their suffering is nearly invisible. As Arlie Hochschild has noted, their care has been fetishized—turned into a private good for sale, abstracted from its context and its origins in the care worker's own family. The true price falls on the head of children in the global South.

If any feminism is going to be worth its name, it will improve the lives of all women instead of setting them in competition with each other or applying only to this or that region or income stratum. Liberal feminism would grant women the right to compete. A radical feminism would grant women a good life in which they have power. It would require a redistribution of care work.

The first step toward gender justice would require a reexamination of the nuclear family. Margaret Thatcher famously declared that "there is no such thing as society. There are individual men and women, and there are families." She was happy to make families the building blocks for her postsociety neoliberal austerity hellscape because they take a number of functions that are common to everyone—child care, housing, food—and privatize them, make them the private responsibility of individual units instead of sites of collective concern and problem-solving.

It is not uncommon today for mainstream politicians to assign moral worth to the two-parent home, preferably with a primary caretaker (implicitly the mother). When presidential candidate Mitt Romney, during a presidential debate, referred to the two-parent home as the best cure for gun violence, he was, preposterous though it may sound, referencing a rich political tradition, often carried by liberal Democrats. Senator Daniel Patrick Moynihan's notorious 1965 report "The Negro Family: The Case for National Action" blamed black poverty on anarchic, matriarchal family structures. President Lyndon Johnson took up this perspective in many of his speeches addressing economic justice. Up through Bill Clinton's welfare policies, George W. Bush's marriage incentives for poor people, and Barack Obama's exhortation to black men to "take responsibility" for their families, this insistence on the two-parent nuclear household as the locus of virtue leaves little room for a more expansive notion of family and care.

The family, however, has rarely looked like this ideal and certainly does not now. The existence of a small nuclear family with a breadwinner and a homemaker became dominant in the United States with the industrial revolution, when home production was replaced with outside work that provided a family wage to the man and assigned housework to the woman. Family structures in other countries and other times have taken many forms—incorporating wide kinship networks, multiple adults in the life of every child, a far more complex definition of households and care than that presumed by the strictures of the American welfare state. Western imperialists, including the British in early America, interrupted matrilineal societies and kinship networks in the name of "modernizing" indigenous people and cramming them into the nuclear family paradigm and new work and welfare patterns.

Since the 1950s, the nuclear structure has been unraveling anyway, hurried along by economic crises that forced women into the labor force, and through women's own desire to enter and succeed in the workplace. The "traditional" family—two undivorced heterosexual parents with biological or adopted children—no longer represents even a majority of families in the United States. We have seen the widely acknowledged feminization of poverty across the globe as the number of single mothers increases without adequate government or social support and no lessening of responsibilities. This sometimes represents a loosening of patriarchy—women can have children without having a man—and simultaneously an increased burden. It is obviously inadequate to keep foisting widely held needs back onto our eclectic range of family structures.

The nuclear family absorbs care responsibilities that concern all of society; the state avoids paying for them, as does business. Men still do little domestic work, wealthy and middle-class women hire people to help with care work, and working-class people make do as best they can. We have a maldistribution of care work that oppresses women up and down the class system. We have a system of anachronistic guilt that makes this hard to talk about. The redistribution of care and the recognition of care work as labor are central to a serious feminist agenda.

This is why universal, twenty-four-hour child care was a primary demand of the 1970 Women's Strike for Equality and must be a first step toward women's freedom. Universal child care seems like a simple goal, but it runs counter to all the strictures thrust on mothers by politicians trying to please constituents at women's expense. When politicians want to cut welfare, they complain about mothers who stay home and don't work. When they pander to family values they worry aloud that mothers are abandoning their roles as full-time nurturers. This has led to the widespread condemnation of the most obvious step toward women's equality: universal child care.

Universal child care is a more revolutionary provision than it seems on its face. First, it makes a direct intervention in the exploitive patterns that maldistribute care work geographically. When child care is turned into a purchasable commodity, an unregulated international market sets poor women against each other in a race to the bottom for care work wages in the global North. Second, as Johanna Brenner has noted, in the past "domestic burdens did not keep women from participating in bursts of militant action but they were a barrier to participation in day-to-day organization building," thus marginalizing women's needs in leftist struggles for equality. This leaves unions, for example, battling for higher wages in male-dominated industries while leaving, say, women's reproductive rights (surely as much a factor in autonomy and survival as a higher wage!) off the agenda. Countries with more robust social programs than the United States—France, Germany, Sweden—provide robust child-care options with taxpayer dollars from the moment of birth.

Still, it's no accident that the countries with the strongest social policies are those in which labor has been most historically victorious. When the working class has power, working-class women pursue certain sorts of benefits. Today, in the United States, we can look to Wisconsin. The increased importance of, say, reproductive justice issues in leftist struggles increases when more women are organizing. When Wisconsin governor Scott Walker launched a nearly simultaneous attack on unions and on reproductive health services, women's organizations and labor unions (particularly teachers and nurses who were mostly women) took to the street. They formed a coalition that is carrying on today, tying together reproductive justice and working-class solidarity as twin victims of the vicious right-wing austerity program. There is simply no reason why reproductive justice (the economic and social ability, not just the right, to access birth control, abortion, health information, and so on) should be lower on the agenda than wage increases. Child care facilitates women's pursuit of these political goals.

In the long run, far more collective, community-controlled living arrangements may be desirable to integrate parenting more naturally into the pace of family life. The original Israeli kibbutzim are good, though obviously fraught, examples, communities where children were cared for collectively by adults and were deeply socialized with the other children.

More communal living will require, in part, a debunking of the contemporary celebration of highly individual "natural" motherhood—softly lit descriptions of motherhood transforming women, making them whole, with constant attachment and attention part of the bargain, the implication that a woman's life should be only her child. "An approach that makes biology the source of all virtue condemns, in one sweep, all men as well as women who have not had children," notes French feminist Elisabeth Badinter. "The new naturalism has the ability to generate feelings of guilt that can drive changes in attitudes." The child's physical and psychological well-being is at stake, so what mother wouldn't feel guilty about transgressing contemporary norms of maternal dedication? Badinter counters the movement for long-term breast-feeding, promoted by the La Leche League International and others, with studies that show everything from allergies to IQ unaffected by the use of formula and other feeding technologies.

Her assertion that the "maternal instinct" is largely a bogus concept cooked up to stuff women back in the home was recently backed up with some rather striking evidence: when

Nebraska decriminalized child abandonment in 2008 in an effort to protect newborns, parents started dropping off their children, several over the age of thirteen. One mother drove from California to discard her fourteen-year-old.

Communal child care may not sound like liberation itself, but consider how revolutionary its implications sound in the context of modern American culture. Nina Power cites Toni Morrison in her pamphlet *One-Dimensional Woman*: "I want to take them [teen mothers] all in my arms and say, 'Your baby is beautiful and so are you and, honey, you can do it. And when you want to be a brain surgeon, call me—I will take care of your baby.'" In other words, women's choices are limited by childbirth only because we allow them to be and place the onus on the individual family, rather than on the entire community. But, continues Morrison, "we don't want to pay for it. I don't think anybody cares about unwed mothers unless they're black—or poor. The question is not morality, the question is money. That's what we're upset about."

The ideal of "having it all" reflects, in a sense, a timeline compressed by a capitalist work ethic. Both men and women are, in theory, capable of "having it all," just not all at once. Someone needs to hold the baby. Imagine the deep liberation of pursuing life on one's own timeline without one's womb set in strict opposition to one's work. Imagine there being no "wrong" time to have a baby. And imagine no fear that to have a baby would be to sacrifice the good life that you want that baby to have.

Women's health should be treated according to women's needs and not their income. There are a number of demands specific to women's needs that would surface in a truly sex-equal leftist program. Abortion on demand not just in theory, but in practice, for free, with transportation; serious domestic violence prevention; the ability to parent without ever wondering whether your child will have food; practical control over one's body through information and free care—these are central to a feminist future.

It is not feminist to celebrate a cracked ceiling when it's just one woman, or a handful, raining shards on those in the basement. Gender currently divides the working class—women's struggles are often pushed aside as if they are not half of the population—but it should be central to our struggle, an asset. A set of social rules around the nuclear family has obscured what is possible by thrusting burden and blame back onto women via antiquated notions about care work and responsibility. The world we want to see would be one where women not only control their own bodies, but also where society itself embraces the care of children and transforms a private burden into public collaboration. There is no reason for the human life cycle to turn to the drumbeat of capital, and the liberation of women from that march will recast daily life in a vision of equality.

THE GREEN AND THE RED

Alyssa Battistoni

Four decades after the first Earth Day, everyone's an environmentalist—and yet the environment is in worse shape than ever. Species we hardly knew existed are dying off en masse; oceans are acidifying, in what sounds like the plot of a second-rate horror movie; numerous fisheries are collapsed or on the brink; freshwater supplies are scarce in regions home to half the world's population; agricultural land is exhausted of nutrients; forests are being leveled at staggering rates; and, of course, climate change looms over all.

We're confronted with the fact that human activity has transformed the entire planet in ways that are now threatening the way we inhabit it—some of us far more than others. And the idea that the environment is some entity that can be fixed with a solution is part of the problem. There are lots of different kinds of environmental problems, and their solutions don't always line up: water shortages in Phoenix are a different matter from air pollution in Los Angeles, disappearing wetlands in Louisiana, or growing accumulations of atmospheric carbon. What unites these crises, though, is that they share the challenge posed by environmentalism's familiar old stumbling blocks: consumption and jobs.

Environmentalists have long lectured Americans about using too many natural resources. By now, the talking points on overconsumption are familiar: 5 percent of the world's population uses 25 percent of its resources, and emits about the same percentage of its greenhouse gases; if the whole world lived like Americans, we'd need four planets or maybe five. We eat too much meat, drive too many miles, live in houses that are too big, shop too much for stuff we don't need. When it comes to climate change, our footprint is even worse than the numbers suggest: Western nations outsource a huge percentage of emissions to the places that increasingly produce our goods.

Such international disparities have, of course, presented a challenge to those concerned with both domestic and global justice: by global standards, America's poor are wealthier than most of the world; ergo, they're part of the problem. But while discussions of consumption tend to focus on a universal "we," as epitomized by the famous Pogo Earth Day cartoon—"we have met the enemy, and he is us"—it's important to look more closely within the rich world rather than simply heaping scorn on national averages. Depictions of American consumerism focus on the likes of Walmart and McDonald's, suggesting that blame lies with the ravenous, grasping

masses. Meanwhile, it's easy for the wealthy to appear virtuous, driving Priuses, living in energy-efficient urban apart-
ments, and eating freshly picked organic kale. But it turns
out that whether you care about the environment, believe in
climate change, or agonize over your coffee's origins doesn't
matter as much as your tax bracket and the consumption
habits that go with it.

As Princeton's Stephen Pacala points out with respect to
carbon emissions, "the rich are really spectacular emitters . . .
the top 500 million people (about 8 percent of humanity) emit
half the greenhouse emissions. These people are really rich
by global standards. Every single one of them earns more than
the average American and they also occur in all the countries
of the world." The US Congressional Budget Office estimates
that the carbon footprint of the top quintile is more than three
times that of the bottom. Even in relatively egalitarian Canada,
the top income decile has a mobility footprint nine times that
of the lowest decile, a consumer goods footprint four times
greater, and an overall ecological footprint two and a half
times larger. And as income inequality has grown, consumption disparities have increased accordingly: air travel, for
example, is frequently pegged as one of the most rapidly growing sources of carbon emissions, but it's not because budget
airlines have democratized the skies—rather, flying has really
exploded among the hypermobile affluent.

Still, greater attention to domestic differences and trans-
national trends doesn't eliminate the need to address international disparities. The global wealthy may consume far and
away more than the rest, but global consumption won't level
out by bringing everyone up to even Western median levels;

consumption in rich nations, even at relatively low levels of income, must decline if we're to achieve some measure of global equality. For those in rich countries, this sounds suspiciously close to an argument for austerity: we've been profligate, and now the bill is coming due. That may be easily reconciled with more ascetic strains of environmentalism, and even with certain elements of left critique. But for those who aren't bothered by decadent consumption so much as by the fact that so few are able to enjoy it—not to mention reluctance at recalling Soviet drabness and specters of breadlines—the prospect of limiting consumption is deeply worrisome. It's hard to talk about consumption without a whiff of moralizing disapproval, as if there were something inherently wrong with wanting to have nice things. Thus the condemnations of consumer culture that once occupied social critics have largely fallen out of fashion, seen as too Puritan, too patronizing, too snobbish—and maybe even too boring. We get it already.

But it's important to distinguish between different types of consumption. For all the resonance in the rhetoric of anticonsumerist environmentalism and austerity, reducing public consumption would actually be an environmental disaster. Reductions in public goods tend to produce increases in private consumption: people drive cars instead of taking the bus, move to a house with a yard instead of going to the park, buy books and home entertainment systems instead of going to libraries and museums, drink bottled water instead of tap. That is, if they can afford to. Those who can't, of course, just have to go without. Indeed, it's hard to think of many things more disingenuous than arguing that addressing environmental issues will impose unacceptable restrictions on the American standard of living while simultaneously promoting austerity measures—yet that attitude is pervasive in mainstream political discourse.

But while having stuff doesn't make you a miserable, soulless materialist, as some of the shriller anticonsumerist rhetoric would suggest, there's not much evidence that it makes you happier, either. Rather, the status treadmill frequently does the opposite: fueling anxiety, inadequacy, and debt, all while redistributing money upward to the executives who pocket most of their companies' profits—and all under the banner of democracy and freedom. Meanwhile, consumer guilt has led to an explosion in green products—recycled toilet paper, organic T-shirts, "all-natural" detergents—but most do little more than greenwash the same old stuff while bestowing a sheen of virtue on their users and suggesting that personal choices will save the planet.

The individual agonizing that constitutes consumer politics isn't going to get around the fact that the global economy depends on more or less indefinitely expanding consumption. It's not just workers who are threatened by the argument that consuming less will put millions out of work worldwide and crash the global economy. We all are. Even our trash is creating jobs somewhere.

Indeed, you can't talk about consumption without talking about production—which brings us to jobs, which environmentalists have long been accused of killing. In his essay "Are You an Environmentalist, or Do You Work for a Living?," titled after a bumper sticker seen in a logging community in the Pacific Northwest in the 1990s, the environmental historian

Richard White argues that environmentalists need to think more seriously about the relationship between modern work and nature, which, he argues, "form the most critical elements of our current environmental crisis." To be sure, the history of environmentalism is littered with projects aimed at keeping patches of nature free from human impact, often demonizing those who work in nature in the process. But concern about ecological problems has also animated efforts to rethink that core relationship.

While most Depression-era policies were aimed at boosting consumption, agricultural policy sought instead to reduce production. The Agricultural Adjustment Administration intended to reduce surplus crops by offering farmers economic incentives to cut down on acres planted; when that program was ruled unconstitutional, it was replaced with the Soil Conservation and Domestic Allotment Act, which aimed specifically to address the soil erosion that caused the Dust Bowl by paying farmers not to plant on fragile land. The federal government also instigated a land-purchasing program to permanently remove millions of acres of "submarginal" land from cultivation and place them under public control, resulting in the creation of the National Grasslands.

These programs, designed by technocrats with little concern for equity or social justice, were deeply flawed. "Submarginal" lands were defined as those that weren't profitable enough for the farmers who owned and worked them to afford to implement the recommended soil conservation practices—a policy that essentially penalized smallholders and initiated the move toward the industrial-scale agriculture whose environmental and social effects have been disastrous ever since.

Familiar tensions between economic and environmental goals were visible in the frequent conflicts between emergency relief legislation that mandated hiring the unemployed and the efficiency mandates of soil conservation policies. Most important, New Deal agricultural reforms were surface-level and temporary, and incentives to overproduce were only momentarily stifled. As Donald Worster writes in his history of the Dust Bowl, none of these reforms "touched the core of Great Plains agriculture—its devotion to unlimited expansion and its attendant sense of autonomy from nature." Rather, "conservation as a cultural reform had come to be accepted only where and insofar as it had helped the Plains culture reach its traditional expansionary aims." Once the drought began to subside, production picked up again—and underlying vulnerabilities remained intact.

Yet for all their problems and partiality, these programs suggest different ways of organizing production. The agricultural initiatives instigated in response to the Depression and the Dust Bowl were among the first examples of what's now called "payment for ecosystem services" (PES). While the term encompasses many different types of programs, the general idea is to identify different ecological processes—pollination, say, or soil fertility—and assess them in terms of monetary value. It sounds like a quintessentially neoliberal strategy—and indeed, that's often how it's been deployed. But the ideas originally motivating PES are remarkably similar to those of the radical feminist Wages for Housework movement of the 1970s. Wages for Housework pointed out that capitalism depends on the socially reproductive labor of the household, and by calling that work an act of love, makes it free. By demanding recognition of and payment for household labor, the Wages for Housework movement sought to unsettle assumptions about "women's work," force recognition of undervalued work, and ultimately force a reconsideration of the relationship between reproductive labor and traditional notions of the productive economy.

As with Wages for Housework, in which the concrete demand for payment acted as a provocative starting point, the demand for payment for work done to and by ecosystems was meant as an unsettling metaphor: the first step in a broader project of rethinking the relationship between human society and the natural world it's built on. Payment for Ecosystem Services began as an attempt to value the work that we call nature and take for free: it sought to recognize the natural services that are taken for granted; to acknowledge that livelihoods don't exist separately from environments; and to reject old, often racialized ideas of conservation that emphasize keeping humans out of pristine environments. It gestures toward an economy that recognizes the value of the care given to ecosystems, and the value of the work necessary to sustain life. It can also recognize the value of *not* working in the name of sustainability, as in programs that pay people not to cut down trees—compensating them for income forgone in the name of global sustainability.

At least that's how it was once envisioned. While the PES framework has been deeply uneven in its implementation, it has often served to advance privatization and commodification of the services it claims to protect. The value produced by ecosystems is frequently captured and consolidated by powerful local actors, or translated into tradable commodities such as credits for carbon markets, which have thus far been wildly volatile and failed to achieve either environmental goals or poverty alleviation. PES programs that assign value to ecosystems without attention to equity and ownership often incentivize states or investors to take over suddenly profitable natural assets, dispossessing people of access to subsistence holdings and delivering benefits solely to investors. Meanwhile, dividing ecosystems into packages of services to be traded and sold loses sight of the complexity and interdependence of what's supposedly being preserved. In short, like so many once-promising ideas, Payment for Ecosystem Services has largely been captured by neoliberalism.

But the underlying principles—recognizing the use value of ecosystems, and recognizing that so-called environmental issues can't be separated from questions of livelihood—may still be salvageable. We need to think seriously and expansively about the work that goes into caring for and maintaining ecosystem services—and about the costs that sustainability will impose on individuals and communities. They will likely be more extensive than we tend to think.

To be sure, industry has long taken advantage of the popular stereotype of job-killing tree huggers to resist improving safety and pollution standards, threatening that being forced to install sulfur scrubbers or to properly ventilate work spaces will spell doom for business and put thousands out of work. Those estimates of job loss tend to be wildly exaggerated, while the jobs that industry projects claim to create are vastly overhyped. TransCanada, for example, has claimed that building the Keystone XL tar sands pipeline would create twenty thousand jobs; the State Department projects something more on the order of five thousand—and most of them temporary ones at that. But environmental regulations sometimes do kill jobs within industries, even if on balance they often create more—and sometimes they kill industries altogether. And while nakedly extractive occupations such as coal mining and oil drilling are the standard examples of practices that the shining ecofuture will render obsolete, a closer look implicates less obvious industries and less obvious kinds of work.

A "green economy" can't just be one that makes "green" versions of the same stuff, or one that makes solar panels in addition to Hummers. Eco-Keynesianism in the form of public works projects can be helpful in building light-rail systems, weatherizing homes, and restoring degraded ecosystems—and to be sure, there's a lot of work to be done. But a spike in green jobs doesn't tell us much about how to build an economy that provides for everyone without creating jobs through perpetually expanding productivism. The problem isn't that every detail of the green economy isn't laid out in full—calls for green jobs, which are meant to recognize the fraught history of labor-environmentalist relations and to gesture toward a commitment to making sure that sustainability doesn't come at the expense of workers or working communities. It's that the vision they call forth isn't a projection of the future so much as a reflection of the past—that most visions of a "new economy" look a whole lot like the same old one. They reveal a hope that climate change will be our generation's New Deal or World War II, vaunting us out of hard times into a new era of jobs and widespread prosperity. But the Keynesianism underpinning that vision was the answer to a problem that was identified as underconsumption rather than overproduction: it was intended to jump-start demand rather than reduce supply. If overconsumption is actually the problem, we can't fix it by consuming more, however ecocertified the products.

Indeed, the very idea that green jobs will drive economic recovery is closely tied to notions of continued American hegemony: green tech is the next big thing, the rhetoric goes, and America needs to stay ahead of the pack. But nearly every country in the world harbors similar hopes. That the wealthiest country in the world is so panicked at the prospect that others might catch up bodes ill for the notion that continued growth will somehow reach an end point in which everyone enjoys a decent standard of living; a global race to be the green tech leader may produce some technological breakthroughs, but it's a race without end.

Fortunately, that's not the only way to get there. The mythology surrounding the New Deal often obscures the fact that labor's response to the Depression was not to make more work, but to share existing work more broadly by shifting to a thirty-hour workweek; Keynes himself famously predicted that we'd be down to a fifteen-hour workweek by the end of the twentieth century. The decision to use fiscal policy to stimulate consumption instead was a means to avoiding deeper structural changes—to grow the pie rather than ask who was eating most of it. Since then, instead of increasing leisure time, productivity gains have largely gone to increasing private consumption—and for an increasingly small number of people. These days, of course, many people are having leisure forced upon them—it's frequently employers who are cutting hours and workers who are desperate for more. It's clear that we can meet needs with vastly less labor than was once required—and with vastly less than will support a population dependent on stagnating wages. While neoclassical economists pose the consumption-leisure trade-off as a choice made by individuals, whether people work in the first place is clearly determined by decisions made at a societywide level.

It's beginning to look like we should have taken the other New Deal: we need to explicitly shift toward working less—to reorient the consumption-leisure trade-off toward the latter on a social level—and share the work that remains more evenly. The sociologist Juliet Schor says we could work four-hour days without any decline in the standard of living; similarly, the New Economics Foundation proposes that we could get by on a twenty-one-hour workweek. Meanwhile, David Rosnick and Mark Weisbrot suggest that the United States could cut energy consumption alone by 20 percent by shifting to a schedule more like Western Europe's, with thirty-five-hour workweeks and six weeks of vacation—certainly not a panacea, but hardly impoverishing, either—while in a study of industrialized nations over the past fifty years, Schor, Kyle Knight, and Gene Rosa find that shorter working hours are correlated with smaller ecological footprints.

While making people work demoralizing jobs to earn a living has always been spiteful, it's now starting to seem suicidal; growing economies just so people can "earn" their living is a recipe for disaster. It's time to reclaim job-killing environmentalism, this time not as a project that demonizes workers, or even work—rather, as one that rejects work done for its own sake. Instead of stigmatizing and criminalizing the unemployed and "nonindustrious poor," perhaps we should see them, as David Graeber suggests, as the "pioneers of a new economic order"—one where we all work and consume less, and have more time for other pursuits.

But calls to share work and do less of it aren't quite right either. Addressing environmental issues suggests the need not only for new kinds of jobs but also for new approaches to work altogether. As White points out, no work or human activity, however removed from the land, is without environmental impacts—yet some work is less material-intensive than others. An ecologically viable future will rely on kinds of work that are typically undervalued, or not considered work at all—care work, done for people and ecosystems; education; work that creates services and experiences rather than sales; work that builds communities. There are dangers in romanticizing these kinds of labor, of course: replacing fast food with a return to gardening and canning might just reinstitute a toilsome regime for women. But done right, a reevaluation of work undertaken from an ecological perspective could elevate the unpaid work of making a social world. Proposals to shorten the workweek are often defended on the basis of giving people more time for what they will—to spend with family, write a novel, cook elaborate meals with garden-fresh vegetables, and so on. But calling those activities "leisure" diminishes their importance in making a life with less stuff a worthwhile and fulfilling one. Likewise, the word "leisure" doesn't credit the fact that strong communities are as important for surviving natural disasters as strong seawalls. If we're paying people to build the latter, shouldn't we also pay them to build the former?

In short, we need to divorce income from conventional notions of production, and institute a social wage—perhaps most obviously in the form of a universal basic income. Basic income won't, in and of itself, solve environmental problems; it won't replace coal plants with solar panels or ease pressure on depleted aquifers. But it marks a critical starting point in rethinking the relationships among labor, production, and consumption, without which environmentalism will go nowhere. More pragmatically, in providing an alternative to dependence on destructive industries and removing the threat of job blackmail from communities desperate for livelihoods, it makes change a real option, and it gives workers and communities more power to demand protections against environmental harms. It can start to reorient social focus away from an eternal game of consumption catch-up toward what constitutes a good life. It admittedly won't do much to curb the upper bounds of consumption, but it might point in that direction. Environmentalists often point to World War II for evidence that people will accept restrictions on consumption for the sake of a shared cause, but the so-called Greatest Generation didn't exactly accept their rations with a patriotic grin. What that experience does demonstrate, however, is that while people don't like limiting consumption under any circumstances, what they really don't like is cutting back if everyone else isn't doing the same. That sentiment is typically mobilized in service of antiwelfare politics:

why should I have to work if someone else just gets a check? But during the war, it went the other way: more than 60 percent of the population supported capping incomes at $25,000 a year—a relatively paltry $315,000 today.

Of course, the postwork future has long been over the horizon; to propose it as a solution to such time-sensitive problems may seem wildly, even irresponsibly, utopian. The revolution might happen in time to avoid environmental catastrophe, but we probably shouldn't count on it. But in countries where high unemployment is the norm, basic income doesn't seem so far-fetched: it's a serious demand in South Africa, while pilot projects are under way in Brazil, India, and Namibia. Some African climate activists have put basic income grants, financed by wealthy nations' payment of ecological debt, at the centerpiece of their demands.

In fact, even the United States presents some interesting opportunities. The most prominent progressive alternative to a straight carbon tax or cap-and-trade system is a policy known as tax-and-dividend, in which the proceeds from a carbon tax would be distributed unconditionally to all citizens—similar to the oil dividend paid to every Alaskan resident. It's defended as a compensatory mechanism for the higher energy prices that would result from a carbon tax; in more bluntly political terms, it functions more or less as a bribe to garner support for a tax that would otherwise be unpopular. There are plenty of criticisms to be leveled against the plan as currently designed, particularly if it's considered a stand-alone climate solution—individual dividends won't maintain levees, support public transportation systems, or build affordable urban housing. But it's also a potential wedge into new obligations and relationships: the first suggestion of a guaranteed income for all, financed mostly by a tax on the environmentally destructive consumption habits of the wealthy. It's an assertion of public ownership of the atmosphere, and the staking of a new claim to public resources. Viewed as a wedge into linking an unconditional livelihood provision to environmental sustainability, it could be the beginning of a much larger project of ensuring decent standards of living for all regardless of productive input, while reclaiming environmental commons and public ownership of natural resources from the false yet persistent narrative of paralyzing tragedy.

That may seem overly hopeful about dim prospects. To be sure, it's hard to emphasize enough that this is meant as a suggestion for a general direction rather than a solution per se. While we can draw ideas from past efforts to cope with environmental problems, there are no real precedents for what we now face. More specifically, the fact remains that fossil fuels have unique properties that make them extremely useful, and the world we live in is built atop them; we shouldn't underestimate how difficult it will be to replace them, particularly as the planet itself changes around us. In short, we're going to have to figure some of this out as we go. Dealing with environmental problems will entail changes too numerous to enumerate here—from land-use planning and urban development to immigration and a host of other issues.

Indeed, the effects not only of climate change itself but of adaptation to it threaten to be most damaging to those who have done the least to cause the problem: the new enthusiasm for reshaping urban landscapes in the name of "climateproofing" threatens a return to the days of Robert Moses, complete with the displacement and destruction of communities along familiar racial and class lines; a price on carbon could end up isolating the increasingly working-class suburbs, while the creative class in the rejuvenated urban core pat themselves on the back for their eco-mindedness; growing concern about climate in countries of the North may paradoxically serve to diminish the funds made available for adaptation and mitigation in the global South as governments direct attention to domestic adaptation projects. Equilibrium models that assume a stable base state of "balance" are increasingly recognized as outmoded for economies and ecosystems alike, yet without a commitment to unconditional social provision, talk of resilience, flexibility, and adaptation is all too easily collapsed into justifications of perpetual precarity.

Observing the protests outside the Copenhagen climate summit in 2009 and reflecting on the apparent tension between the recognition of limits cautioned by those claiming "there is no planet B" and the limitlessness implied by chants of "everything for everyone," Michael Hardt suggested the need to "develop a politics of the common that both recognizes the real limits of the earth and fosters our unlimited creative capacities—building unlimited worlds on our limited earth." Virginia Woolf might seem an odd place to turn in response, but her essay "A Room of One's Own," while best known as a seminal piece of feminist polemic, could serve just as well as a manifesto for such a politics. In it, she reflects on the "instinct for possession, the rage for acquisition," which keeps "the stockbroker and the great barrister going indoors to make money and more money and more money when it is a fact that five hundred pounds a year will keep one alive in the sunshine." With those five hundred pounds, she wrote, came the freedom to think and write as she pleased. We might add a few more things to the list—say, universal health care and a bus pass—but figuring out what it takes to keep all seven-billion-plus people on the planet alive in the sunshine is the fundamental task of the twenty-first century.

The postwork future is often characterized as a vision of a postscarcity society. But the dream of freedom from waged labor and self-realization beyond work suddenly looks less like utopia than necessity; divorcing individual consumption from production is looking more and more like the only way to live decently in the face of resource constraints. And so there's no more important time to ditch the moral value attached to consumption, and the link between consumption and desert—without simply running in the opposite direction and valorizing consumption for its own sake. Perhaps in the postpostscarcity society, somewhere between fears of generalized scarcity and dreams of generalized decadence, we can have the things we never quite managed in the time of supposed abundance: enough for everyone, and time for what we will.

RED INNOVATION

Tony Smith

The technological dynamism of capitalism has always been a powerful argument in its defense. But one of its secrets is that at the heart of this dynamism we find no bold entrepreneurs, no venture capitalists, no established firms.

Investments pushing the frontiers of scientific knowledge are just too risky. The advances sought may not be forthcoming. Those that do occur may never be commercially viable. Any potentially profitable results that do arise may take decades to make any money. And when they finally do, there are no guarantees initial investors will appropriate most of the resulting windfall.

There is, accordingly, a powerful tendency for private capital to systematically underinvest in long-term research and development. Despite popular perceptions that private entrepreneurs drive technological innovation, the leading regions of the global economy do not leave the most important stages of technological change to private investors. These costs are socialized.

In the quarter-century after World War II, the high profits garnered by American corporations due to their exceptional place in the world market allowed corporate labs to engage in "blue-skies research" projects. But even then, public funding accounted for roughly two-thirds of all research and development expenditures in the United States, creating the foundations for the high-tech sectors of today.

With the rise of competition from Japanese and European capital in the 1970s, private-sector funding of research and development increased. However, long-term projects were almost entirely abandoned in favor of product development and applied-research projects promising commercial advantages in the short-to-medium term.

Basic research continued to be funded by the government, like the work in molecular biology that supported the move of agribusiness companies into biotechnology. The same was true for projects of special interest to the Pentagon—the developments associated with the Defense Advanced Research Projects Agency, for instance, which paved the way for modern global positioning systems—and other government agencies.

But medium-to-long-term R&D in general was in great danger of falling into a "valley of death" between basic research and immediate development, with neither the government nor private capital providing significant funding for it.

For all their rhetoric touting the "magic of the market-place," those in the Reagan administration recognized market failure when they saw it. They began to offer federal and publicly funded university laboratories various carrots and sticks to undertake long-term R&D for US capital.

New programs were created to provide start-ups with resources to develop innovations prior to the "proof of concept" required by venture capitalists. Under Reagan, the Small Business Innovation Development Act even mandated that federal agencies set aside a percentage of their R&D budget to fund research by small firms. These and other forms of public-private partnership have granted US capital enormous competitive advantages in the world market.

It's no surprise that Apple's tremendously successful lines of products—iPads, iPhones, and iPods—incorporate twelve key innovations. All twelve (central processing units, dynamic random-access memory, hard-drive discs, liquid-crystal displays, batteries, digital single processing, the Internet, the HTTP and HTML languages, cellular networks, GPS system, and voice-user AI programs) were developed by publicly funded research and development projects.

It hasn't been the dynamics of the market so much as active state intervention that has fueled technological change.

THE PROMISED GOLDEN AGE

Technology is more than just a weapon for inter-capitalist competition; it is a weapon in struggles between capital and labor. Technological changes that create unemployment, de-skill the workforce, and enable one sector of the workforce to be played against another shift the balance of power in capital's favor. Given this asymmetry, advances in productivity that could reduce work time while expanding real wages lead instead to forced layoffs, increasing stress for those still employed and eroding real wages.

Two ongoing technological developments further strengthen the power of capital. Advances in transportation and communication now enable production and distribution chains to be extended across the globe, allowing capital to implement "divide and conquer" strategies against labor to an unprecedented extent.

Astounding new labor-saving machines are also becoming more and more inexpensive. A recent exhaustive study of over seven hundred occupations concluded that no less than 47 percent of employment in the United States is at high risk of being automated within two decades. Anything approaching this level of labor displacement will yield more misery, not progress, for ordinary workers.

But the lower cost and higher capacities of machines have also led to change of a better sort. As the prices of computer hardware, software, and Internet connections have declined, many people can now create new "knowledge products" without working for big capitalists.

Multitudes across the globe now freely choose to contribute to collective innovation projects of interest to them, outside the relationship of capital and wage labor. The resulting products can now be distributed as unlimited free goods to anyone who wishes to use them, rather than being scarce commodities sold for profit.

It is beyond dispute that this new form of social labor has generated innovations superior in quality and scale to the output of capitalist firms. These innovations also tend to be qualitatively different.

While technological developments in capitalism primarily address the wants and needs of those with disposable income, open-source projects can mobilize creative energies to address areas capital systematically neglects, such as developing seeds for poor farmers or medicines for those without the money to buy existing medications. The potential of this new form of collective social labor to address pressing social needs across the globe is historically unprecedented.

In order to flourish, however, open-source innovation requires free access to existing knowledge goods. Leading capital firms, hoping to extend their ability to privately profit from publicly supported research, have used their immense political power to expand the intellectual property rights regime in scope and enforcement, severely restricting the access open-source projects require. Copyright, after all, was extended for twenty years at the turn of the century, just as Internet access was starting to balloon.

Despite these barriers, the success of open-source projects shows that intellectual-property rights are not required for innovation. Further evidence is provided by the fact that most scientific and technological workers engaged in innovation are forced to sign away intellectual property rights as a condition of employment. These rights actually hamper advancement by raising the cost of engaging in the production of new knowledge, and by diverting funds to unproductive legal costs.

THE WORLD IS FLAT?

Capitalism also hampers the ability of much of the world to contribute to technological advancement. Whole regions of the global economy lack the wealth to support meaningful innovation. Today, only four countries spend over 3 percent of their GDP on research and development; a mere six others devote 2 percent or more.

Capital in these advantaged regions has the opportunity to establish a virtuous circle, free-riding on the extensive public investment discussed above. Privileged access to advanced R&D enables capitalists to appropriate high returns on successful innovations; these returns allow those companies to make effective use of technological advances in the next cycle, setting the stage for future profits.

At the same time, enterprises in poorer regions, lacking access to high-level R&D, find themselves trapped in a vicious cycle. Their present inability to make significant innovations that would enable them to compete successfully in world markets undercuts their future prospects. Only a handful of countries—such as South Korea and Taiwan—have ever been able to move forward from this starting disadvantage.

Global disparities in technological change alone do not explain why 1 percent of people in the world now own 48 percent of global wealth. But they are a major part of the story; technological change is a weapon that enables the privileged to maintain and extend their global advantages over time.

CREATIVE NON-DESTRUCTION

The destructive effects examined above are not necessary features of technological change; they are necessary features of technological change in capitalism. Overcoming them requires overcoming capitalism, even if we only have a provisional sense of what that might mean.

The pernicious tendencies associated with technological change in capitalist workplaces are rooted in a structure where managers are agents of the owners of the firm's assets, with a fiduciary duty to further their private interests.

But a society's means of production are not goods for personal consumption, like a toothbrush. The material reproduction of society is an inherently public matter, as the technological development of capitalism itself, resting on public funds, confirms. Capital markets, where private claims to productive resources are bought and sold, treat public power as if it were just another item for personal use. They can, and should, be totally done away with.

Large-scale productive enterprises should instead be acknowledged as a distinct type of public property, and exercises of authority within these workplaces as acts of public authority. The principle of democracy must then come into play: all exercises of this authority must be subject to the consent of those impacted by it.

Though additional regulations would be needed if managers were elected and subject to recall by the workforce as a whole, technological advances in productivity would not typically result in the involuntary unemployment of some and the overwork of others, but rather in reduced work for all.

We know this because workers say they want more time to spend with their families and friends, or on projects of their own choosing. With democracy in the workplace, the drive to introduce de-skilling technologies would be replaced with a search for ways to make work more interesting and creative.

Suppose that decisions regarding the general level of new investment were also a matter for public debate, eventually decided by a democratic body. If there were pressing social needs, the overall rate of new investment could be increased; if this were not the case, it could be stabilized. These bodies could then set aside a portion of new investment funds to provide public goods free of charge, putting more useful goods and services outside the market's reach.

The public goods of scientific and technological knowledge resulting from basic research and long-term R&D would be decommodified, too, as would the fruits of open-source innovation. The latter could be unleashed by abolishing intellectual property rights and by providing an adequate basic income to all—enabling anyone who wished to participate in open-source projects to do so. If special incentives were required, generous prizes could be awarded to the first to solve important challenges.

Remaining funds could then be distributed to other elected bodies at various geographical levels, each of which would determine what share would go to public goods in a region.

The remainder would be distributed to local community banks charged with allocating them to worker enterprises.

Various qualitative and quantitative measures could be employed to measure the extent to which those enterprises used technologies to meet social wants and needs effectively, with the results determining the income beyond the basic level received by their members (and the members of the community banks that allocated investment funds to them).

Abolishing intellectual property rights would have the added benefit of ensuring that wealthy regions could not use technological knowledge as a weapon to create and reproduce inequality in the global economy. This danger would be all but eliminated if every region were granted a fundamental right to its per capita share of new investment funds.

Finally, if workplaces used productivity advances to free up time for their workers rather than to increase the output of commodities, resources would be depleted and waste generated at a much lower rate. Abolishing capital markets and replacing them with democratic control over levels of new investment would free humanity from the "grow or die" imperative and the environmental consequences that follow from it.

If enterprises were acknowledged as inherently matters of public concern, it would eliminate the obscene absurdity of having the fate of humanity rest on whether profit-driven oil companies have the political and cultural power to extract and sell an estimated $20 trillion of fossil-fuel reserves, as they clearly plan to do.

If open-source innovation flourished, the creative energies of collective social labor across the planet could be mobilized to address environmental challenges. If poor regions with fragile ecologies were guaranteed their fair share of new investment funds, the pressure to sacrifice long-term sustainability for the sake of short-term growth would be overcome.

Of course, all of these proposals are vague and provisional. Nonetheless, they show that the social consequences of technological change could be far different than they are today. We do not need private ownership of productive assets, or markets devoted to financial assets, to have a technologically dynamic society. With the necessary political shifts, technological change would no longer be associated with overaccumulation, financial crises, the stifling of open-source innovation, severe global inequality, or the increasingly palpable threat of environmental catastrophe.

We need to unleash the full potential of human ingenuity. The way technology advances is already socialized in important, if restricted and inadequate, ways. We can finish the job and make sure that its fruits are put to the benefit of ordinary people.

THE CURE FOR BAD SCIENCE

Llewellyn Hinkes-Jones

Current scientific research is said to have drifted toward Pasteur's quadrant. Otherwise known as "use-inspired basic research," it is a reference to how esteemed French biologist Louis Pasteur never took on a scientific study that had no real-world application.

In his work, Pasteur was trying to further the cause of science and general understanding of the universe, but he made his decisions of what to study based on the potential for future applications. He wasn't just investigating the unknown; he was investigating the unknown causes of important public health concerns. Such a focus would eventually lead him to construct the germ theory of disease, whose implications were vast, changing the scope of medical science for years to come.

The term Pasteur's quadrant comes from the 1997 book of

the same name by Donald E. Stokes, which espoused use-inspired research as a way to drive innovation. Stokes's book was a stark contrast to the staid philosophy determined by Vannevar Bush more than a century ago that scientific research should be divided between basic research (toward greater understanding of the world) and applied research (toward direct applications of said knowledge).

Stokes believed that use-inspired research, similar to that of Pasteur, could be the best of both possible worlds. It would drive research for the public's benefit, expand our understanding of the world, and justify science budgets in an age of austerity.

If scientists could focus their research based on real-world applications of that research, more innovative discoveries could be developed quicker and more efficiently.

Use-inspired research can certainly be a good thing. Pasteur's contributions to science alone prove its merit. But emphasizing utility as a requirement for science budgets undermines the basics of science. Basic research, the kind aimed at furthering human understanding without real-world applications in mind, is a necessity. Without it, there is a void left where all scientists must defend their actions with cost-benefit analysis.

Not all research fits so easily into a category of immediate utility. Bohr's research on the structure of the atom would eventually have untold applications, but few at the time would have been able to predict what those applications would be. If anything, most major scientific discoveries of the past century were premised on basic research whose applications were yet to be determined. Pasteur is largely the exception.

Utility is often in the eye of the beholder, and not all problems are as straightforward as finding the cure for a disease or predicting the next earthquake. Yet, in our age of austerity, science must often provide its own reason for existing. Such a shortsighted dependence on utility eventually corrupts science. If science has to be immediately useful, how accurate does it need to be? Does it need to be true or just beneficial? Or does it just need to feel right?

If anything, the current scientific world and its overwhelming number of retractions have transcended Pasteur's quadrant into what might be termed the TED Talk quadrant. Funding is increasingly driven by an attention-driven enthusiasm for what is compelling and potentially revolutionary for First World problems.

What entertains an audience is not necessarily what is best for science. The needs of the scientific community are not necessarily those that make for an inspiring performance. Not all problems can even be simplified into a five-minute oratory. Sometimes the solutions are rather boring. They don't so much involve curing cancer as discovering a new mechanism for hormone receptor treatments that may one day lead to curing one type of cancer.

This emphasis on quick and easy revolutionary solutions takes its toll on the science being done. The heightened race for grants only encourages more inaccuracy and shortsightedness to keep up with every other groundbreaking study that is about to revolutionize the world.

Good science is still being funded. New advancements, from cutting-edge treatments for hepatitis C to replacement limb surgery and the ever-advancing march of computing technology, are all pushing the boundaries of our understanding. But there is a lot of funded science that isn't. The race to cure cancer and heart disease has inspired thousands of potentially earth-shattering discoveries, but only a fraction of those have held up. Heavily cited studies about the mathematics of positivity have gone on to earn acclaim, sell thousands of books, garner TED Talks, and get more funding for research even though the original study had major errors.[1]

All the while, private interests, especially in the world of biotech, exert undue influence over what research gets funded and what the results of that research say. Neuroscience offers cures to almost any disease of the mind, while much of the social sciences have completely lost their mooring. It may not seem dire from the outside, but it is a tragedy in slow motion that has grand implications for the future.

It is an urgent call to reinforce basic research and move away from the quadrants of Pasteur and TED Talks. But this is not so simple as saying science should focus on general research. It is necessary to counteract the free-market approach to discovery that has undermined academic research in the past three decades. Neoliberal policies and austerity budgets that drove academic funding to such a use-inspired approach have to be inverted. The framework for state-sponsored, socially beneficial scientific research still exists, but it has been eaten away at the edges. It is just a matter of reversing the privatization of research.

Thankfully, we are far away from the days when Reagan attempted to entirely eliminate the NIH's budget. The NIH is a shining example of how research can be directed and coordinated at the federal level. But agencies such as the NIH continually struggle for their budgets. Combating the privatization of scientific research involves reaffirming financial support for those agencies that already fund basic research.

If anything, their budgets may need to be extended to rein in the flood of retractions. It has only been thanks to a handful of researchers, professors, and concerned investigators that we are cognizant of what has been occurring, and their work needs to be extended.

Researchers such as John P. A. Ioannidis, Paula Stephan, the Reproducibility Project, and Retraction Watch have all made great strides into identifying the root causes of flawed science. Together they and others make up what could be considered an internal affairs of academic research, or what Ioannidis calls meta-research, that didn't previously exist. The newly minted Meta-Research Innovation Center at Stanford aims to continue this avenue of investigation, but if it is true that in 2010 $200 billion was wasted on studies that were "flawed in their design, redundant, never published, or poorly reported" then there is still much more work to be done.[2]

Reproducibility may be one of the least sexy fields of study, as it never leads to international fame. There's little chance of discovering a new cure for cancer by reproducing someone else's work. Results only either reaffirm what was already known or cast doubt on our current knowledge. It does not readily attract the eyes and pocketbooks of private benefactors looking to change the world and cure malaria. It's rarely associated with use-inspired research because its utility is not immediately obvious.

Yet, reproducibility is an essential part of basic research. Without it, science has a weakened claim to objectivity. If studies aren't reproduced, mistakes and errors are presumed to be accurate. This is why more funding will have to be directed at replication. Because of its less than exciting nature and to ensure independence from conflicts of interest, that funding will most likely have to come from the state.

Part of the effort to eliminate flawed research is the need to stem the pernicious tide of publication bias. Otherwise known as cherry picking, it gives a misrepresentation of research findings toward the interest of a more exciting result. Studies that don't shatter the earth or revolutionize how we think about disease get buried in the dustbin.

Not just publication bias; there are an unlimited number of other ways by which science can be contorted into what its handlers want it to be, and the solution to most of them is increased transparency. Government-funded grants should require that all data and findings be released at the conclusion of a study. All clinical trial data should be released for access to FDA approval of a drug. Studies should be registered beforehand to avoid the "Texas sharpshooter's fallacy" (selecting a conclusion after the fact). There should be a detailed list of standards and practices for all government-funded research. This might include anything from minimal sample sizes to proper analytical methodology.

Right now, science journals are a hodgepodge of private organizations dependent on advertising for funding and dependent on their subscribers for collective oversight. Such a free-market approach to science publishing leaves them open to corruptive influence. They should provide easy and low-cost access to their archives to improve the transfer of knowledge that will encourage more oversight. There also needs to

be certification for journals, or some variant thereof, to separate respected peer-reviewed science journals from predatory
publications eager to fleece scientists and publish unreliable
results.

Many of these resolutions are aimed at curing the supply
of faulty science that gets published, but there is still the ever-
growing demand to err with research that needs to be
addressed. At the heart of this problem is the race for grants
and attention that underlies the funding of the academic
research system.

States have been constantly slashing funding for education
over the past two decades, leaving universities to foot the bill
through higher tuition costs, selling patents, private dona-
tions, and investments through endowments. Being without
a stable source of funding takes its toll on academic research.
To get money to fund their work, scientists need to continually outdo each other with more explosive discoveries to
attract more funding. It is a race for grant money that only
encourages cutting corners.

To eliminate this rush for grants and attention means
shoring up public university finances. Stable financing would
mean that more focus could be put toward basic research, replication, or any other necessary variety of science that doesn't
garner headlines or chase patents without depending on private financing from pharmaceutical companies.

Simultaneously, too many postdocs are graduating into a
field that cannot sustain their employment, and there is a race
for the few staff scientist positions that exist. Such a cutthroat
competition for careers only encourages sloppy research.

Postdocs who have little leverage in such a tight labor market are less willing to speak out about flawed experiments and less likely to encourage unexciting results.

More staff scientist positions need to be created to eliminate what Dr. Paula Stephan called the "pyramid scheme for employment." As well, more limits need to be put on how many postdocs can be accepted if the job market can't sustain their employment once they graduate. Just because a university is in need of tuition and low-wage lab workers shouldn't mean that it should take on an unending supply of willing students.

A reform of the academic labor market requires wholesale change to ensure that there is full employment for staff scientists and universal basic income for others. Otherwise the competition for well-regarded, high-income positions will always be vicious.

The combination of defunding public universities and the liberalization of patents through Bayh-Dole has turned the academic research system into a research arm of private industry that is still subsidized by the state. To denude private industry's influence over academic research may eventually mean reversal of Bayh-Dole so that state-funded research remains in the public interest rather than a lottery ticket for schools hoping to win big by patenting DNA sequences.

Such reforms constitute an overhaul of the academic system. Scientific research and the public university system are connected at the hip, and there is little recourse to separating them. Addressing issues of scientific integrity not only involves implementing standards and practices of science publishing but also addressing the academic process as a whole, particularly skyrocketing tuition costs.

Students who take on insurmountable debt for a career in science are unlikely to do anything that might risk their future prospects. They are less likely to question the bounds of their research or blow a whistle when things go wrong.

Academic reform should be a major issue, but it currently isn't. The baffling number of retractions may cause scandals for those professors caught manipulating data, but the deep tragedy is that bad science doesn't lead to outrage. Unless they happen in large quantities, retractions usually appear quietly and then disappear into the background, which is reasonable. Quiet retractions are meant to protect honest mistakes from destroying careers and unnecessarily shaming innocent parties.

But the burden of such inauspicious retractions is left on the general public, who won't recognize the slow erosion of objective knowledge. They quietly accept dubious nutritional claims on food packaging long after they have been rebuked in the world of science. They don't notice the lack of progress in combating uncommon diseases. It is only when an obscure disease such as Ebola makes headway into the United States that there is a scramble to patch up holes in our understanding and to race for a cure.

But such outbreaks provide an opportunity to counteract the spread of bad science. Shining a critical light on the world of scientific research gives the public a chance to see how the sausage gets made. It provides an insight into the scientific process outside of the enthusiastic praise for potential discoveries regularly found in the news media. It opens a dialogue to question how federal science grants are being used. And potentially, it offers an opportunity for reform of the grant system, to reestablish federal influence over research, and to move away from Pasteur's quadrant.

If anything, Pasteur's quadrant of use-inspired research is akin to a capitalist approach to science. In the purest form of use-based research, science would only be conducted when it was needed. Like a privatized police force, it would only serve those who were able to pay and at the last second. Diseases that affect the downtrodden would be ignored. Decisions would not be made by the scientific community but by independent researchers and their funders. Balding cures would get more funding than those for malaria.

Not just economic, this is a deeply epistemological debate that questions whether science is simply a tool to be used whenever emergencies arise, or an essential part of our daily lives. Does it matter if the general public understands what omega-3 fatty acids are and how they work, or is it all consumer propaganda meant to influence purchasing habits? Does it matter that the epidemic of "crack babies" never really existed and that it was a moral panic based on a single flawed scientific study?

Is scientific truth a fluid concept fungible to our whims, or is it a necessary part of our objective understanding of the world? Is science an arcane language for an elite class to make political decisions, or is a Deweyian scientific cast of mind an integral aspect to democratic thought?

If the answer is the latter and an educated populace is a necessary element of a just society, then there are large-scale social reforms that need to happen to achieve those ends.

There is a great opportunity to replace the current kludged system of state universities and their research arms with a wholesale scientific establishment. Rather than scientists racing each other for attention and employment, it would be one dedicated to the pursuit of objective knowledge that no longer needs to constantly justify itself in financial terms.

FINDING THE FUTURE OF CRIMINAL JUSTICE

In March 2015, the Schomburg Center for Research in Black Culture, a division of the New York Public Library, convened a panel discussion, "American Policing: Lessons on Resistance," to discuss the organizational response to police brutality and racial discrimination. Participants in the debate—activists and community leaders—also articulated the demands of communities across the country and laid out visions of a just society and the changes needed to achieve one in the United States.

MODERATOR:

Mychal Denzel Smith. A contributing writer for *The Nation* and thenation.com and a Knobler Fellow at The Nation Institute,

Smith is a freelance writer and social commentator. His work on race, politics, social justice, pop culture, hip-hop, feminism, and black male identity has appeared in various publications, including *Ebony*, *theGrio*, *the Root*, *Huffington Post*, and *GOOD*.

PANELISTS:

Ashley Yates is an activist, poet, and artist raised in Florissant, Missouri, who is also cocreator of Millennial Activist United.

Dante Barry is the executive director of the Million Hoodies Movement for Justice.

Phillip Agnew is the executive director and cofounder of the Dream Defenders, a community activist group of minority youth who have been recognized as the next generation of civil rights leaders.

Cherrell Carruthers is a national organizer for Equal Justice USA.

MYCHAL DENZEL SMITH: Good evening. I want to set out some intentions up front. I don't want anyone in this room to mistake me for an objective or impartial journalist-moderator. I have marched with organizers and organized with everyone on this stage. I am, I feel, as much a part of the movement as

I am a recorder of it. I have an agenda, and that agenda goes back to the idea of a third reconstruction, the first being obviously the Reconstruction era after the Civil War, the second being the civil rights movement. For me, to get to reconstruction, there must be the abolition of something, there must be the destruction of something, and to my mind that means if we are to be in a third reconstruction we need to pull down the pillars of white supremacy and I believe that the police are one of those. I would like to see the abolition of the police.

I believe that black Americans exist in a police state. I believe, as James Baldwin wrote in 1966, that the police are simply hired enemies of this population. They are present to keep the Negro in his place and to protect white business interests and they have no other function. I believe that if we're talking about a movement to end police brutality we have to acknowledge the fact that by social decree and political will the police are violent by necessity. That is the function of their job, so if we're talking about ending police brutality, I believe we're talking about ending the police. So my first question: is this a movement toward police abolition?

CHERRELL CARRUTHERS: It is. We have to put this movement in the context of other historical movements. We need to understand that what's going on today is a part of five hundred years of struggle and resistance. It didn't start or stop with the civil rights movement. So we talk about antislavery, we talk about antilynching, we talk about anti–Jim Crow— we have to put this in the context of five hundred years of resistance. I say that discriminatory policing happens because it is part of a system that is historically racist, and so we have to dismantle the police state.

PHILLIP AGNEW: I fully agree. This is a movement to end the police and the system of policing, and we should root the discussion in the true history of police in this country. Historically, the police have been used to quash labor disputes, keep black people from veering outside of their designated areas, police drunkenness, prostitution, and vagrancy, and make sure that people were ready to go to work. It is easy to see that if we are to create a movement for liberation it must mean the ending of police as we know it. But I think the discussion should rather be about what justice is in our communities, what that looks like, not what policing in our communities should look like.

DANTE BARRY: A lot of the sentiment has been that we are in a new civil rights movement. When we also look at the 1960s civil rights movement, that was about certain access to power, certain types of rights, and being able to see the election of a President Obama. This current movement is not about that type of access to power. We recognize that even with a black president the power structure is not working. So this movement is also about transforming power and creating a completely different society than the one we have today. So when we say that black lives matter, that is a political demand, it's an actual vision for what we are fighting for. So the movement wants to answer these specific questions: What does the world look like when black lives matter? What does education look like when black lives matter? What does health care look like when black lives matter?

ASHLEY YATES: I don't know if I would necessarily say that this movement is about ending the police, but it is about ending the police as it stands, in the way they operate in our communities, the way we've been indoctrinated to believe police are supposed to interact with our communities. It's about reframing that, reshaping that, rethinking what order should look like in our society and who really benefits from the order that's been imposed on us. It's important that we go back and examine the historical context. Slave patrols were actually drafts of sorts, right? So the only people who were able to sign up for them, who were required to sign up for them, were white males age six and up. That's the beginning of the structure we live in today, so we can understand why it doesn't work for us. We shouldn't force ourselves to think in binaries, of a police state or a state with no police, but really to think about what policing means when it benefits everyone, when black lives matter, and what policing means in terms of keeping order that benefits everyone in society.

MDS: So does an armed police force fit into the idea of a world where black lives matter?

AY: Consensus? Okay.

DB: It's not just policing, but also the surveillance state and the incarceration state. It looks like a three-legged stool. Each part of the prison-industrial complex works and feeds into

each other, so I think we're talking about completely dismantling the PIC.

CC: I'm thinking about what safe communities look like. If
everyone was to close their eyes for a few seconds, just for a
few seconds indulge me, and go to a place that is secure and
warm, who is around you? What does it look like? Who is
there with you? Now raise your hand if there was a jail cell in
your vision, a security camera, a police force. Any hands?
No. So, in this neoliberal context we define safety and security by surveillance, by cameras, police, resource officers in
the schools. When we imagine a safer community, we need
to redefine what safety and security are outside of these policies like broken windows policing and vertical patrols. So
when we talk about justice, we have to imagine what safety
is for us. What does that look like? What does that mean?

PA: Policing gives weight to capitalism. If you did not strip
people of every faculty, every ability to raise themselves up
from the muck, from the sewer, and force them to do things
that they otherwise would not do if they had the means to put
food on their tables and provide for their basic necessities, then
you would not need a police force. When we look at the history of police departments, their expansion across the country
did not correspond or correlate with an increase in crime.
Nor did the war on drugs or Jim Crow or the period right
after slavery, when conscription into chain gangs escalated.
None of those correlated with an increase in crime, but with
a need for more black labor, with a need to control the movement of black people or poor people, with the need to further

separate poor white people from poor black people. So in the world that we want to see, the counterweight to capitalism means we not only eliminate police, but also the things that generate and build crime, which are poverty, having one class of people who have everything and live in abundance and then a mass of people who live in scarcity.

MDS: Absolutely, but there are things we can do now and policies we can fight for, issues we can organize around that will remove the police from aspects of our lives or deny them access to the amount of force they're using. So what are some of those things we can do right now?

DB: Most immediately, Million Hoodies is working on a campaign to demilitarize police, but not just in terms of equipment. This stems from the war on drugs, the war on terrorism, and how black, brown, and Arab communities are continuously affected by militarized policing practices, technology, and equipment, which includes surveillance, police, and incarceration. On a national level, there is a bill being proposed around the Stop Militarizing Act. That's one immediate way. But also just looking at your local communities and if you're on a college campus, particularly—more than 130 college campus police departments have access to 1033, the bill that allows federal surpluses of military equipment, tanks, and tear gas on college campuses—private, public, community colleges, even high schools. There's a trajectory in terms of the school-to-prison pipeline that's creating a zero-tolerance police practice in Arab, brown, and black communities, from the school to the community. Locally we need to think about the practices, the equipment, and the technology that militarize the police, like SWAT, who killed Aiyana Jones, a seven-year-old black girl in Detroit, and really push back against that.

AY: The first step is demilitarizing the police, but not only in equipment, also in culture. The police are in our black and brown communities, but why are they there? Because we've been criminalized. If we start looking at the policies, we see the things that have been criminalized and notice that they're usually circumstances that occur in black and brown communities—that's how we get to broken windows policing. We also have to look at our school system and how they've started to criminalize us as people very early on. We're seeing our kids not only being suspended, not only being taken out of school, but also convicted of crimes that occurred within the schools, so they're entered into the system early. Once they get back to their neighborhood, they're criminalized. Deconstructing the process of who's criminalized and also the response in terms of the militarization of the police and how they're accultured to act in black communities and what we think of as crime—that's a big part of it, too.

PA: New York has a model of cop watch that should be elevated and discussed intentionally around the country. I think the only way you're going to balance the overreach that runs rampant in police departments around the country, the culture of contempt and disdain for black and brown people, especially when they're young and poor, the only way to stop or even stem the killing of our people is to present a counterweight. Right now the faculty we have, or the agency, is to be able to monitor the police and watch them. It's not the end-all, be-all. Absolutely not. We've had a lot of talk about police cameras and their ability to save us, but I just don't believe it. We've got to fix training, we've got to increase accountability, we've got to make sure there are some real consequences and repercussions when somebody takes someone from our community. We've got to make sure they feel it in their pockets every time somebody sues the city and wins. At the moment, that money comes from us. We pay the damn lawsuit.

A mentor of mine said any demand we put forward should be framed in terms of whether person blank would still be alive if this demand had been in place. If the demand wouldn't have kept person blank alive, then why are we making it? That's what we should operate from.

DB: There's actually a reinvestment in police going on. In New York City right now police commissioner Bill Bratton has proposed an extra one thousand to six thousand new cops on the street, and that's in response to a decline in crime.

MDS: I mean, there's a historical analogy here, right? SWAT teams were formed in response to the Watts rebellion. This has happened before. We see an uprising, we see the empowerment of people, and then we see this state response.

CC: A lot of these issues have been going on for decades. This didn't start in August 2014 in Ferguson. It's really interesting that when something like this happens, legislatures come out and decide to create solutions, as if this weren't already a problem. About demilitarization, the ACLU put out a report that in the past two years there've been more than eight hundred uses of SWAT teams with militarized weaponry. About 80 percent of those are for nonemergency arrests, usually drug-related. Only about 7 percent of those were emergencies, and those usually involved white assailants, while the drug offenses usually involved black and brown communities. We also need to divest from those who profit from private prisons. The private prison industry is a billion-dollar entity. Some of your favorite brands—Victoria's Secret, Target—profit from private prison labor. So we need to look at how capitalism has made it profitable for us to criminalize black and brown communities, so much so that these companies come in with their lockup quota. So you have people who have no interest in reforming or dismantling the system when they're literally profiting off it.

MDS: In California they recently passed Prop 47, which reclassifies a lot of low-level nonviolent felonies as misdemeanors, and that means getting people out of prisons. It also means that future arrests will not result in a felony conviction on things like credit card fraud, possession of stolen goods, and marijuana possession. And the money that's being saved from not prosecuting these crimes is being invested into the school system and mental health care. So is that a model we can follow, and how do we do that? What would an organization like Dream Defenders do in terms of following that model and getting something like Prop 47 passed?

PA: For us the equivalent is focusing on the fight against private prisons. In Florida 100 percent of our juvenile prisons are private, and they're moving to privatize all of the adult prisons. In Florida 346 inmates were murdered last year in jail. If we're working in a reform frame and we've got to win something now for our survival, then better to just forget the whole system, don't call the police, and when they come in, make sure they leave. We need to make sure folks know that for every child who fails the FCAT in third grade, they have an algorithm saying they'll build a police cell for that child. They need to know that calling the police on their grandson may not be the first option because we've had kids getting murdered in the boot camp, in the diversion program that's supposed to help them. If you're looking at this in an organizing way, private prisons are a particular evil. They may only make up less than maybe 14 percent of all prisons, so they're not dominant. Most of our prisons are still public, but the private institutions are traded on Wall Street. What happens on Wall Street is that you bet on the success of a company, and the success of these companies is based on how many black men and women and poor people they can arrest. This is money that is directly linked to incarceration and the murder of black people. We haven't progressed much; the system's only gotten more slick.

CC: I want to add that privatization is happening in public prisons. They're outsourcing who cooks the food, the programs there, the phone companies.

MDS: Is decriminalization of sex work on the agenda? I ask this question because a lot of the way that we talk about police violence is in terms of what happens to young black men. But we know young black women are shot and killed by police as well, and laws around the illegality of sex work in particular have been used to harass black women, especially black trans women. Is that something on the agenda in terms of moving forward to get police out of our lives?

AY: Absolutely. We have to think about what's deemed criminal, right? We have to think about whether that's something that is actually criminal to us as a society or if it's something we've been taught is criminal. That applies to the legalization of weed and what that means, and also when we think about sex work and who's affected and who's criminalized by that. We have to look at who are oppressed by these laws and who they pull into the system and whether the state has decided that sex work is not a valid way to make a living because those people are more profitable in prison.

It's really about thinking about how we reinvest power, how we reform what we think of as power. And a lot of that is tied to the dollar. As long as it's more profitable to enter mass amounts of black and brown people and poor folks into a system, into prison, then they are going to keep doing it. So what does it look like when we take those dollars away from these companies? What does it look like when we start to pinpoint the people who are profiting from prisons and we affect their pockets? We need to think about these contracts the prisons have and really go about attacking them. It has to be a well-rounded approach. So I think the decriminalization of sex work, the decriminalization of drugs, come with the divestment from the prisons. We have to make them not profitable. It all works together, it's all tied into each other, and that's why this is a movement. It's not just about people who are doing antipolice work, or educational work, it's about how all these pieces fit together.

MDS: Last week, FBI director James Comey gave a speech at Georgetown University that some people have called historic because a sitting FBI director addressed race and law enforcement. I have a number of issues with the speech itself, but I want to point to one thing in particular. In this speech he invoked My Brother's Keeper,[1] and he essentially asked why so many black men are in jail. He's saying that it's not the police's fault, that's not what's going on here. The answer he came up with: "The truth is that what really needs fixing is something only a few like President Obama are willing to speak about perhaps because it is so daunting a task. Through the My Brother's Keeper Initiative, the president is addressing the disproportionate challenge faced by young men of color. This initiative and others like it is about doing the hard work to grow drug-resistant and violence-resistant kids, especially in communities of color, so they never become a part of the officers' life experience." Ashley, you cowrote a piece [with Rachel Gilmer] about why My Brother's Keeper is actually a roadblock, an impediment, to talking about these types of issues. Can you explain what you all were getting at?

AY: Listen, when we say solidarity, that's not just a buzzword, it's not just a word we throw out there to make people feel good about caring about black lives. We highlight the word "solidarity" because the systems that oppress the people who

are on the margins of the margins—systems that are working exactly as they were meant to—also suck other people
into them as well. Some of these systems were intentionally
meant to criminalize black people and were then utilized to
criminalize people just outside the margins of the margins,
and they work their way inward, into society. So we all have
to tackle these systems. Programs like My Brother's Keeper
try to section us off and don't really highlight the intersections
and don't allow us to address the real issues, which are
antiblack sentiment and racial justice. We're talking about a
framework that makes it comfortable for other people to
push aside, you know, Dante and Phil, and say, "Well, they're
actually the problem, they're a subsector of society, they're
like a special breed of black people that we really need to
tackle, because if we tackle this issue then society will be better." The reality is that when *they* tackle the issue they've
imposed upon us, then society will be better. It's basically blam-
ing the oppressed for their oppression. Let's say that black communities have to have black fathers. Let's look at why you've
removed black fathers from our families. Let's look at how that
happened. Let's look at why there's a lack of black men in our
families. Let's look at the things that have been criminalized
and how you've broken apart the black family. So when you
have My Brother's Keeper, which leaves out everyone except
black men, it allows society at large to point a finger at them
and blame them for their own problems. That derails the movement at large and deforms what justice actually looks like,
because just as Phil or Dante can get swept into these policies
that have been made to oppress black people, a white man can
get sucked into them as well. Although they weren't meant for

you they can still be applied to you. When you realize that, then we really can work together to break down some of these systems. My Brother's Keeper imposes solutions that aren't really solutions and doesn't allow us to do that.

PA: Stokely Carmichael said, "Can a man condemn himself to death?" If our government and the system that governs us were to convict Darren Wilson,[2] they would be convicting and condemning themselves. That is too hard to do. If they were to place the blame appropriately they would be condemning themselves—thus, we would hope, predicting their suicide. They cannot do that. And so you've got to blame somebody, and who do you blame? The very people who are the victims of many of your policies. You make them feel like they're solely responsible for what happens to them. Then you parade FBI folks, you parade exceptional Negroes and rappers and entertainers out in front of them who say, "Listen, this is about us. If we get ourselves together, everything will be all right." And this places people in a state of dissonance, a continual tug and pull: What am I doing wrong? This is insidious, it's very seductive, easy to say, "Look at them, I can do it, I can pull myself up." But like I said, can the system condemn itself? No. It refuses to do because the moment that it does, hopefully, through some real organizing, it would be the precursor to its destruction.

CC: Thinking about Comey's speech and about My Brother's Keeper, I'm afraid that we're going to get too excited about some of the respectability politics latent in the speech. White supremacy is a system and Comey spoke a lot about racial bias and racist people, but he did not talk about the policies informed by white supremacy and racism, such as broken windows policing, such as stop and frisk, such as vertical patrolling? All these policies were created to curb the violence and crime that happen in subpar areas with subpar conditions, instead of actually thinking about fixing the subpar conditions in the areas to begin with. And you can come from a two-parent home, you can go to a four-year university, get a master's degree, code-switch, be brilliant, but a degree and a résumé aren't going to stop a bullet, right? You can still get pulled over and profiled. We saw this with Henry Louis Gates, so being a respectable Negro does not stop you from being racially profiled or gunned down by the police. That's what Comey doesn't touch on, that's what My Brother's Keeper doesn't touch on.

Q: First of all, my name is Angelo, and I'd like to thank you all for the symposium you're putting on. My question is, how can we go about starting a political party? Because neither the Republicans nor the Democrats represent us, they keep putting policies together to keep prosecuting us. How can we get all of us in our own lanes to combine as one to do something different?

AY: One of the projects that people are taking up across the nation is the implementation of people's assemblies. What will it look like when we build with each other and stop relying on the existing systems, these political parties, to implement solutions and real growth in our communities? What if we start building our own food co-ops, working with our black farmers, gardening in our own communities, if we do all of these things to build our own power and stop relying on the power structure as it exists? It may not look like what we expect. You might not be able to go to the ballot and check the People's Assembly, but if you get active in your community and start building power within, that's another way to counter the political two-party system.

PA: And run against Democrats, just start primarying against Democrats. Even if you don't win. We're planning a bumper sticker that says: "Don't March, Run." Everybody should run for office. Some of us will lose, most of us will lose, but we'll start primarying against Democrats and make them afraid, because right now Democrats don't fear us at all. We've been there since they fake-freed us.

CC: That's another thing. If you grew up black, poor, progressive like me, you've been told to vote Democrat all your life. The three men most visibly responsible for the repression and pain of those people in Ferguson, they're all Democrats, and I just want to name that.

Q: I come from a marketing and media background and I know how the image of blackness has been configured in white eyes out of fear, out of maybe guilt. Do you think it's worth an educational system to reconfigure white minds with black history, with the real black struggle and what we actually go through daily? I don't feel like in the educational system they actually see the reality of what we actually go through. Is it worth it? Is it needed?

AY: I definitely think it's work that needs to be done. We have to make it so that it's less easy for them to ignore us and ignore our existence, right? Because that's a form of violence. That's erasure, pretending that someone doesn't exist while at the same time you're actively oppressing them. That's part of making sure that the things we're doing out in the streets are working together with the efforts we're mounting in other places. So we do things like Black Brunch,[3] which was started in Oakland, things like taking it to areas where people have sectioned themselves off to feel comfortable and feel like a world that actually exists doesn't really exist, we go in there and say the names of people we have lost from state violence, we put it in front of their faces, and we say, "Oh, my God, I'm sorry, do you not like this loud disruption?" Well, we don't like jump-out crews in our neighborhoods. We don't like stop and frisk in our neighborhoods. We're not comfortable in our streets, so you're not going to be able to drink your mimosas in peace. That has to happen with history books as well.

DB: Part of our job is also to change hearts and minds. This is also a war of ideas, a cultural war just as much as it is a social and political war. Media particularly have a big role in how people perceive black people. We've grown up in a culture where there's a criminal black person on TV and there's a white law enforcement vigilante hero. That's a binary presented from Cops to Law and Order to CSI, all these different shows that perpetuate the same idea. So we need to resist that and disrupt it in every sense, every part of the structure that is designed to not protect us.

CC: It is our job, it is our duty to make those who would have us be comfortable in our oppression uncomfortable. And we do that by educating, by telling our stories, by not erasing our history.

PA: One part of that—either it runs parallel or comes after—is to say to white people, I know it's hard for you to understand, but did you know that you're getting screwed? Did you know that you're getting screwed over as well? Did you know that the first slave revolts were with white and black people? Did you know that you've been accepted marginally into whiteness, but that if you don't wake up, capitalism will come for you, too? It is a wildfire that will take anything in its wake. You've been tricked and duped for four hundred years to think that you are better by virtue of your whiteness.

Q: You all kind of touched on the idea that loving yourself is something that is definitely revolutionary. I know that it won't stop you from getting gunned down, but in your opinion what role does black self-esteem play? Why is it important, and what does it do for us in the movement?

PA: So I grew up poor, I grew up on the South Side of Chicago, and my parents did everything they could to survive. But I grew up with a self-image that was just flawed, just really messed up. It still kind of creeps into my psyche a little bit. It's hard to really get away from it, you know. But the moments when I felt most powerful were in church. I'm not a church-going person anymore, but it was those times when I felt limitless or that I was a part of a community or that my belief in something greater than myself could make the earth quake, and that was revolutionary to me. I felt like I could do anything. Other times are when I'm in the movement. That love and esteem grow and I'm able to silence what I've told myself all these years or what I was told and repeated to myself over and over. Self-esteem or lack of it is very, very crucial to the movement. If we do not love ourselves, our organizations will crumble. That was the first attack, the first way to break a slave. You knew you had broken somebody when you had broken their spirit. So we're talking about spiritual warfare, you know.

CC: There's an Audre Lorde quote, I'm going to paraphrase here, "Self-care is not self-indulgence, it's an act of political warfare." And that's powerful. Black self-love is radical, it's sustaining. In a system that tells you you're nothing and you decide anyway to survive, that's an act of warfare.

Q: The police have gone overtime to try to kill this movement, and the question that's facing us all is how we're going to stop them from crushing people with these arrests. They've rounded people up in their homes for being part of these protests and I myself am facing years in jail for being part of these protests. I've been singled out and targeted by the police. There was a conference in Atlanta, where people whose children had been killed by the police, people who've been incarcerated and activists, got together and they came up with a plan. For one day they would shut shit down everywhere. No school, no work, no business as usual, don't spend any money, a nationwide day of protest following, you know, weeks and weeks of buildup. I'm with the Revolution Club and I want you all to speak to what you think about this.

AY: That's hugely important and I think once again for me it goes back to building up that support with our communities, right? I'll give a prime example. I've been in Oakland for the past couple of months and I don't know how many people are familiar with the protest that was done on Black Friday, but the Black Friday Fourteen were a group of young activists, all women or trans folks, queer folks of color, who shut down the BART so that you were unable to get from West Oakland to East Oakland, which made it impossible for folks to do their shopping and pissed a lot of people off, frankly. There was a real backlash from the people who profit from those trains running, and they tried to crack down, tried to claim $70,000 in restitution, then they tried to ask for community service from the activists, which was laughable. What started happening is that the community really rallied around and said, not only are you not going to receive any restitution, not one dime, not only are you not going to receive any community service from people who are actually trying to make our community better, but also we're going to come into your spaces and make sure that you're being held accountable every step of the way until these charges are dropped. So the BART board has not been able to run business as usual, they have not been able to have a meeting, they have not been able to go to the community spaces and try to disrupt them, they have not been able to have closed-door meetings, which is how they like to conduct their meetings. No, they're going to have to bring everything out into the open and we're going to work on these resolutions together. The community actually passed a resolution to recommend to the DA to drop all the charges. So we have to support the people who are going out and doing the work, so they know there's a community behind them that makes sure they'll be able to sustain it.

AFTER GAY MARRIAGE

Kate Redburn

When the Supreme Court delivered its ruling in June 2015 confirming marriage equality, it was greeted as an historic civil rights achievement. Over the past several years, mounting marriage victories combined with a cresting wave of trans activism had already pushed legal advocates to think beyond gay marriage, the issue that has absorbed the bulk of the movement's advocacy, resources, and powers of mass mobilization. From the legalization of homosexual assembly to the repeal of anti-sodomy laws and now national gay marriage, legal gains for LGBT people since World War II have brought important benefits and legitimized the citizenship rights of people who are not straight or cisgender. It remains true, however, that despite improving attitudes toward gay marriage, LGBT people continue to suffer economic marginalization and violence. Mainstream advocates for gay rights must now join the calls that queer and trans critics have been making for decades to the agenda from "legal equality to lived equality."

Marriage equality critics tend to separate the national legal organizations from more local, community-based work by describing the former as "the mainstream LGBT movement" or "Gay, Inc." Urvashi Vaid, a community organizer and veteran attorney for LGBT rights, suggested that a more fruitful distinction might instead look at the strategies being pursued within and between different organizations at all levels of reach, separating the fight for formal legal equality from a broader analysis of inequality. Looked at from this point of view, it becomes less interesting to ask what a legal organization will do next and more important to evaluate the weaknesses of the gay marriage campaign and identify a new strategy for queer liberation. Although the gay marriage campaign has achieved many of its goals, eliminating a key site of homophobic discrimination and glossing gay relationships with the patina of legal legitimacy, the legal strategy also relied on promoting a narrow vision of gay life mostly constrained to the partnered white cisgender male. Proponents have argued that greater public sympathy leads to legal and social change, but having won gay marriage nationally, the queer and trans youth, elders, immigrants, and people of color still face disproportionate poverty and violence.

The crescendo of trans voices over just the past year has highlighted this inequity and demanded that the movement not only address trans issues directly, but attend to the needs of homeless youth, isolated elders, low-income, and immigrant

LGBT people. Bamby Salcedo, president of the TransLatin@ Coalition, a national organization devoted to addressing the needs of trans Latin immigrant communities, feels that "the focus needs to shift. In our community we're actually getting killed. And there's no additional investment from LGB organizations about the importance of addressing the structural violence that trans people continue to experience." As of July 2015, at least ten trans women were murdered in the United States; in 2014, twelve such killings were reported.

Salcedo brought these issues to Creating Change, the nation's largest LGBT advocacy conference. With a group of protesters, she stormed the stage to prevent Denver mayor Michael Hancock from touting the city's LGBT record just two weeks after a queer Latina teenager was gunned down by police. Salcedo explained that the protesters also hoped to draw attention to the dearth of trans people in leadership of LGBT organizations and to the lack of funding streams for the issues that most affect their communities. If the movement is going to use the LGBT acronym, "the T should be included equally in terms of programming, in terms of services, in terms of funding allocation, in terms of resources allocation," she explained.

A survey of 101 trans Latina immigrant women conducted by Salcedo and the TransLatin@ Coalition found extremely low rates of employment and health insurance coverage and high rates of employment discrimination and poverty. Forty-one percent of respondents listed accessing safe and affordable housing as "very difficult," while 45 percent described feeling "no support" from local authorities. Although the survey has a relatively small reach, the extent of marginalization is staggering. According to the National Transgender Discrimination Survey, trans people are twice as likely as cisgender Americans to live in extreme poverty, a multiplier that jumps to seven for Latin trans people. These results bolster a recent study by the Williams Institute showing consistently higher rates of poverty among lesbian, gay, and bisexual people. It also demonstrated the racialization of queer poverty with evidence that African-American gay male couples are six times more likely to be poor than their white counterparts.

It is true that a marriage contract carries an array of benefits, some of which are financial. Indeed, the argument that gay people should have equal access to those benefits has been the movement's central plank. But there's a problem: if marriage benefits shouldn't depend on sexual orientation, why should they depend on relationship status? It makes basic components of survival like housing and health care contingent on marriage, when they should be accessible to all people, regardless of whom or how they love. The movement has focused on a campaign that treats marriage as an end in itself, instead of as one path to access housing and health-care privileges. William Eskridge, a professor at Yale Law School and an expert on LGBT law, agrees, commenting that "We also need to take this as an opportunity to interrogate and fight for the rights of people who do not want to get married, which includes a lot of LGBT people." Premising the distribution of these rights on marriage legitimizes barriers to access that needn't exist.

The problem is not the marriage litigation itself, but that it has been prioritized at the expense of directly battling economic inequality and violence. Successful litigation can be a

powerful tool for changing political momentum and legiti-
mating new social norms. Eskridge believes *Goodridge v.*
Department of Public Health, the Massachusetts case that led to
the first legally recognized gay marriage ceremonies in 2004,
had an enormous effect outside the courtroom. "Courts can
reverse the burden of political inertia," he said. "Before
Goodridge, to get gay marriage in Massachusetts you'd have to
persuade the legislature and then Governor Romney. *Goodridge*
said no, the default rule is now marriage." The Republicans
failed to rally against the decision, and the holding stood. At
the time, public opinion was starkly against gay marriage.

Eskridge also cited the fact that "courts can give wind to
your social movement by validating your norms." The discourse of rights has enormous purchase in the public arena,
where it can be invoked in more creative ways than the
courtroom allows, if nothing else than as official validation
of the representations the social movement makes about itself.
Framing the debate as one over regular people's right to get
married, raise a family, and participate in the job market makes
it much harder for opponents to rely on tropes about gay
deviance and predation. As Eskridge elaborated, "a court victory can create the conditions for falsification of stereotypes."

At the same time, the litigation strategy has emphasized
gay relationships that don't challenge other social biases by
choosing plaintiffs who are white and partnered. At a book
talk for the Center for LGBTQ Studies (CLAGS) at CUNY
Graduate Center in January 2014, Vaid explained that the
power of law to change norms is a double-edged sword because
"the mainstream movement's imagined subject remains
white middle-class more often male than not and gay." At

be improved with rights alone, but only through a radical redistribution of wealth and power.

The result is a political climate where support for gay marriage is an empty shibboleth, a test of progressive values without disrupting the status quo. Consider the massive outcry over the proposed Religious Freedom Restoration Acts (RFRA) in Indiana and Arkansas. Although RFRA did not add any additional anti-gay discrimination to state laws, the appearance of doing so caused a major public relations disaster in both states. Some of the most publicized support for gay rights came from corporations who do business in those states, including Salesforce, whose CEO promptly canceled all company travel to Indiana. In Arkansas, Walmart won nationwide acclaim for opposing the proposed RFRA bill. But opposing RFRA in Arkansas cost Walmart nothing; in fact it distracted attention from the lawsuit the company is facing for denying partner health-care benefits to a lesbian employee's wife undergoing costly treatments for cancer in a state where gay marriage is legal. Under cover of supportive rhetoric, Walmart is denying sexual equality.

Twenty years ago, a Democratic president was able to pass the Defense of Marriage Act against only a small pocket of dissent, notably coming from civil rights legend John Lewis. Today, twenty-two states ban discrimination against LGBT people, and all states are obliged to allow same-sex marriage. The tides have shifted, and cities, states, and corporations throughout the country vocally support a version of gay rights. Yet a 2015 Harris poll commissioned by Gay and Lesbian Advocates and Defenders (GLAD) showed startlingly high negative attitudes toward LGBT people: a full third of respondents said they would be uncomfortable attending a gay wedding, the same percentage that would be uncomfortable seeing a same-sex couple holding hands, learning that a family member is gay, or learning that one's doctor is gay. This snapshot of public opinion shows how much more work is left to be done.

Thankfully, the past two years in particular have been a period of remarkable growth for grassroots organizing that prioritizes queer and trans people of color. Much of the positive momentum is coming from outside the traditional boundaries of the LGBT movement, from the Black Lives Matter movement in particular. "Black Lives Matter is pushing the LGBT movement to think more deeply about intersectionality and deepen our commitment to that work," contends Janson Wu, executive director of Gay and Lesbian Advocates and Defenders (GLAD).

Queer issues are already integral to these youth-led movements, but the LGBT legal organizations have not historically been so receptive to questions of race and class. Two new constellations of advocacy have emerged to address this imbalance. The fledgling LGBT Federal Criminal Justice Policy Working Group is "aiming to put the broad range of criminal justice issues on the LGBT agenda" and has brought together a wide range of organizations to push for administrative changes to criminal justice. Their first comprehensive report includes detailed recommendations for reform in prisons, immigration policy, and law enforcement, as well as in areas of criminalization for youth, trans people, and people living with HIV/AIDS, from foster care to sex work. A second new initiative, called the LGBT Poverty Collaborative, also seeks to coordinate efforts of service providers, community organizations, and research institutes currently seeking to reduce LGBT poverty. As Vaid sees it, "Very few queer organizations are involved in tax bills or weighing in on the way that public financing has been cut." Economic and social disempowerment are linked and could be dramatically reduced if the gay marriage machine directed energy at broader policies affecting economic inequality.

There is no shortage of alternative models to fund. GLAD was one of the earliest sponsors of same-sex marriage litigation, and yet it defies the binary between pursuing formal equality and broader social justice. In 2013, the organization filed a suit on behalf of a teenage transgender woman who was denied access to both the women's and men's dormitories in a Massachusetts homeless shelter, forcing her to sleep on a mat on the floor of a storage closet. GLAD considers this important suit just one part of a larger intervention in the treatment of trans youth in homeless shelters. GLAD's Janson Wu explained that "We know that policies are just words on a paper or binders on a shelf that can collect dust, and so much of our work is also making sure that those new victories are actually implemented and enforced." In this case, that has included a know-your-rights educational tour for homeless transgender youth, attorney testimony before the Boston City Council, and distribution of a best practices guide called *Shelter for All Genders*. Wu noted that trans visibility is better than ever before, with the advent of the Trans Day of Visibility and Trans 100 list.

Some communities have already organized responses to violence that resist invoking law enforcement at all, using the restorative or transformative justice model to reduce violence outside the confines of the carceral state in recognition that strategies of containment and incarceration serve to replicate, not diminish, violence. Safe Outside the System of the Audre Lorde Project and Streetwise and Safe in New York, as well as Community United Against Violence in San Francisco organize and educate queer and trans communities to prevent violence without calling police. These organizations are part of a growing cohort within the LGBT constellation that seek ways to reduce intimate and state violence within a prison abolitionist framework. In stark contrast to the legal reasoning that advocates for increased penalties for hate crimes and discrimination, these organizations join the Black Lives Matter call to see the criminal justice system as a target for change, not an ally for protection.

The stakes are nothing less than the legacy of the gay marriage campaign. Will it be the first step toward lived equality, or will it neutralize queer and trans difference into a homonormative parody? GLAD's Wu told me, "I think we have a real opportunity and I think there's a real risk that our community may lose interest." At the moment, only 4 percent of LGBT people donate to the cause, a sign of economic marginalization and of how much work remains in mobilizing our communities. It's also an opportunity for queer and trans people to drive the movement toward connecting with ongoing struggles to raise the minimum wage, build affordable housing, promote reproductive justice, and end mass incarceration. Winning these campaigns could be a critical first step toward queer and trans liberation.

In January 1965, A. Philip Randolph declared that the civil

rights movement faced a "crisis of victory." A decade had passed since *Brown*, two years since the March on Washington, and Randolph was convinced that racial justice would only come through more radical change. Three short months later, his movement compatriots would begin to march from Selma to Montgomery, meeting violent resistance at the Edmund Pettus Bridge and prompting the Voting Rights Act, once ranked the most successful piece of civil rights legislation in American history.

Fifty years later the first black president stood by that bridge and laid claim to a progressive tradition by declaring, "We're the gay Americans whose blood ran in the streets of San Francisco and New York, just as blood ran down this bridge." Queer and trans Americans face our own crisis of victory: whether to accept Obama's analogy, his implication that racism and homophobia have been conquered, or to use the successes of the past to launch a renewed effort to defeat economic inequality and endemic violence.

SMALL, NOT BEAUTIFUL

Tim Barker

Writing in *Good* magazine, journalist Nona Willis Arono-witz, a self-styled progressive, announced a new social move-ment for young people concerned about the recession. "We should all be mobilizing for the mobile food movement." We should "fight" for street carts threatened by city ordi-nances. Aronowitz is quick to admit that street food is often unhealthy, and with the low prices she attributes, there's no way the cart owners can provide generous employee bene-fits. Why, then, do we owe the food carts such indulgence? Because, Aronowitz writes, "you're supporting a small busi-ness owner at a corporate fast-food price point."

Since I enjoy street-cart falafel with unhealthy regularity, I understand where she's coming from. But something in Willis Aronowitz's management theory–inflected prose (what the hell is a "price point"?) gave me pause. We're supposed to cheer when one of her protagonists, a recent Cornell graduate who was able to secure tens of thousands in start-up capital from family connections, starts "regularly turning a profit" on his food cart. Why are the heroes of this new "movement" budding capitalists? The only answer is that the businesses in question are small. Apparently the conflict between management and labor—instinctually familiar to any young person who has worked a terrible job—is contingent on the size of the company in question.

This is not an uncommon view. Its adherents include everyone from Barack Obama, who says that small businesses are "central to our identity as a nation," to the radical Seven Stories Press, which augments its translations of Zapatista agitprop with the claim that small business represents "everything you want to fight for." Many leftists and liberals believe that small businesses are a politically significant phenomenon, and a positive one at that. Their critique is of "big business" or "corporations" instead of capitalism itself.

The scale of a business is viewed as a stand-in for its virtue. By this logic, a multinational corporation such as Walmart is more worthy of ire than a locally owned bodega employing fewer people, charging higher prices to its working-class clientele, and paying less to its workers (or paying nothing to the young family members who often find themselves "helping out"). The "mobile food movement" readily falls into the small business slot, and so, unhealthy food and low wages aside, we should be "fighting for" its scrappy entrepreneurs.

The problems with the small-business fetish fall into two general categories. First, the celebration of small business ignores the advantages provided by centralization and concentration. Larger companies, run by efficiency-focused managers and able to support human resources bureaucracies, have also often been well in advance of small businesses in matters of civil rights, benefits, and workplace safety issues. This isn't, of course, because big capitalists are virtuous; rather, their relative insulation from day-to-day market upheavals and their well-developed legal staffs make it easier for them to adapt to federal regulations than Mom and Pop can. They're also more likely to be unionized. Small businesses often operate on tighter profit margins, leaving them especially vulnerable to market pressures and eager to cut costs—especially the cost of human labor. The greatest gains in unionization came in those centralized factories—such as River Rouge in Detroit—where massive scale and oligopolistic profits emboldened worker initiative and enabled management flexibility. Moreover, small businesses aren't capable of generating the productivity gains that have enabled the American economy to produce more social wealth with less resources and less labor time. Supporters like to claim that small businesses create disproportionate numbers of new jobs, but the volatile small business sector also destroys most jobs, leaving the net effect unremarkable. According to a report from the US Census Bureau, "In a nutshell, net job creation . . . exhibits no strong or simple relationship to employer size."

It's precisely because small businesses are marginal to the broad currents of American economic life that progressive hopes invested in them are so misguided. In the general context, they can't help but be inextricably dependent on bigger businesses. Say you put your money in a local credit union, hoping that your deposits will sustain local businesses. The bank's business, whatever its size, is to make money from your money by investing it. But odds are that your local economy lacks profitable ventures sufficient for all the money it has on its hand. What happens next? The money gets passed to a big bank such as Chase, and from there it can go anywhere—bankrolling corporate raiders, funding environmentally disastrous expansions overseas, supporting companies that kill union organizers.

Writing in the wake of the recent financial crisis, Doug Henwood, one of the sharpest left critics of the small business myth, recently gave empirical weight to these reservations. Looking up "local" alternatives to Citibank and Bank of America in his own Brooklyn zip code, Henwood found one's assets to be heavily invested in the US government and another to be bankrolling the gentrification of New York's outer boroughs. And what goes for banks goes just as well for other small enterprises, which inevitably deposit their money somewhere where it will be sent on a global chase for the best return. These connections also vitiate many of the supposed environmental benefits of buying locally. Even among radical environmentalists, it is a matter of debate whether buying from a local bookstore is really better than ordering online. To get to your favorite small business, most things have to be shipped or trucked, and of course they sit in stores that run air-conditioning and lights (probably powered by burning coal). Global capitalism is a dense and tangled net. Few commodities, no matter where you buy them, present true political alternatives.

Second, the fetish for small business endorses a deeply flawed ideology of human fulfillment. It implies that true fulfillment is achieved through the ownership and command of property and people. It simultaneously denies the importance of empowering the majority of people who find themselves among the commanded. By posing the issue as one of big business against small, it cedes pride of place in the struggle for social justice to managers instead of workers. And in small-businessmen, we find a particularly unreliable group of progressives, to say the least. Take the example of Chris Doeblin, owner of a small bookshop in one of New York City's university neighborhoods. Liberal-minded professors recommend that students patronize his local business instead of the Barnes & Noble–operated university bookstore, and the store survives on these professors' loyalty to the small business ideal.

Unfortunately, Doeblin—a leading evangelist of the "inherent good one does in shopping at local indies"—has a long history of conflicts with his employees. Faced with overwhelming union-mediated complaints about wage theft and health-care benefits, he flatly told the *Columbia Daily Spectator* that "The only tool I have to stay afloat is to cut payroll." Regarding health care, another manager said, "We just can't do that for everyone." Doeblin even told the press how much he'd love to bust the union, and not only for fiscal reasons. "Along with the financial constraints it places on his business, 'one develops a terrific sense of entitlement.'" These words are chilling but accurate reminders that "the inherent good one does in shopping at local indies" does not extend across class lines.

What's more, Doeblin's direct testimony reveals the brutal individualist ethos that survives in small-business owners. "If you don't want me to be as dedicated to running business as I am," he says, "fine, go shop at Walmart." Rather than appealing to social justice or environmental rhetoric, he appeals to a competitive sense of entrepreneurial mastery. They see themselves as owners of a fief, dependent on their own extraordinary personal talents, and thereby justify arbitrary and unilateral control of the workplace. To such people, unions can only be divisive distractions that keep workers from realizing that their true interests are best understood by the benevolent, farseeing owner himself. A worker's desire to join a union is seen as an egregious "sense of entitlement"— precisely the language a lord might use in condemning an uppity vassal.

Such attitudes are more than anecdotal. Businesses that sell locally have proven themselves quite capable of thinking and acting nationally. Take the National Federation of Independent Business, a small-business lobby that claims hundreds of thousands of members. The NFIB donates 95 percent of its PAC money to Republicans, and its legislative priorities have included opposing the Family and Medical Leave Act, the Americans with Disabilities Act, and the Employee Free Choice Act. (There is, to be fair, a liberal counterpart to the NFIB, but it counts less than a tenth of the NFIB's membership. This makes sense: in one study, randomly selected small-business owners displayed a similarly conservative profile to random NFIB members.)

Now, make no mistake: Mexican food *is* better at hole-in-the-wall taquerias than it is at Taco Bell; browsing at a charming little bookstore *is* more fun than doing it online. But the politics of small is better is so insidious precisely because it allows aesthetic or consumer qualities such as these to stand in for real politics, allowing liberal shoppers a countercultural thrill while leaving basic economic structures unchanged. The point is not to deny that we enjoy certain small businesses but to acknowledge that, politically speaking, this matters about as much as our preference in necktie patterns.

In his extravagantly subtitled book *Rebel Bookseller: Why Indie Businesses Represent Everything You Want to Fight For, from Free Speech to Buying Local to Building Communities*, Andrew Laties declares proudly of his own ilk: "Booksellers are autonomous. We pursue opportunities as our capacities permit." A noble idea! Why shouldn't human needs and desires shape the economic world, rather than vice versa? But Laties limits this claim for autonomy to a small, privileged class to which he—and his union-hating confreres such as Chris Doeblin—already belong. And this class is not a group, such as those who possess adequate health care, which happens to be small but could be expanded. Rather, it is a group that is *necessarily* small. Everyone can't be a small-business owner. Every boss needs employees to manage. The ideal of richly rewarding autonomous work is distorted beyond recognition when wrung through the ideological filter of the small-business fetish—we continue to glorify full and free employment but embed it in a context that demands most people lose the game and forfeit the right to a living wage or adequate benefits.

Likewise, opposition to "big business" can reflect admirable and understandable feelings—the protest against opacity, control of important decisions by a small, unaccountable group, and obvious barriers to class mobility is a protest against capitalism, not yet conscious of itself as such. And the arguments against lionizing small businesses should not be misconstrued as arguments in favor of big businesses, which we all know perpetrate similar sins on a larger scale. But the economy cannot be neatly divided into "good" and "bad," "big" and "small" capitalisms—the problems go deeper and require fundamental renovation rather than delicate pruning. An economy based on small local businesses wouldn't work, but even if it could, why would we want it? Instead of counterpoising good owners to bad owners, and leaving most people frozen out, we should articulate a new vision of a world without bosses, where *everyone* pursues opportunities as their capacities permit. A thousand little fiefdoms won't cut it.

Of course, if small is no guarantee of virtue, neither is big any guard against vice. A future run by McDonald's or Walmart isn't worth fighting for—in fact, the entrenched power of those corporations is a big reason for the problems of the present. Widespread enthusiasm for small business, however misguided, reflects a healthy understanding of the specific pathologies that can affect large enterprises, whether in the workplace (big companies investing in expensive shift-scheduling software that prevents workers from being able to plan their lives in advance) or in public (where huge concentrations of wealth are regularly converted into illegitimate power over "democratic" politics).

For socialists, the problems with large and small businesses share a common source—the private ownership of productive wealth and the unchecked power that employers exercise over workers as a result. The size of an enterprise is ultimately less important than the larger structures that condition and constrain everyone who lives and works in a given society. This conclusion may sound pessimistic when applied to our capitalist present, but it also means that radicals can allow themselves to be creatively agnostic about the shape and size of future alternatives.

For example, a publicly administered investment fund could finance the gradual transformation of small businesses into cooperatives owned by the people who work there, who could then exploit the potential that small-scale organizations offer for face-to-face relationships and direct participation in decision-making. Consumer cooperatives, in which neighbors work collectively to fulfill the needs they share, offer another way to preserve the local ethos we associate with small business. Alternatives to wage labor, such as a guaranteed basic income (paid to everyone whether they worked or not), could provide an economic buffer for even more radical experiments, including the production and transfer of certain goods and services without any exchange of money at all.

Local solutions like these will have to find their way experimentally and gradually, and they will never offer a full-fledged alternative form of life without complementary programs that need to be administered on a bigger scale. But even many of these grander projects—such as guaranteed high-quality education, medicine, and child care—will work better if implemented to allow for maximum community involvement. We would all do well to heed historian Daniel Immerwahr's recent call for "a left that can operate on all scales," one that would refuse the dangerous illusion that local knowledge is always right without being willfully blind to the fact that small really can be very beautiful.

THE RED AND THE BLACK

Seth Ackerman

One of the most fundamental reasons the left has historically been suspicious of detailed visions for an alternative social system, apart from avoidance of a kind of technocratic elitism, is that such visions have so often been presented as historical *end points*, and end points will always be disappointing. The notion that history will reach some final destination where social conflict will disappear and politics come to a close has long been a misguided leftist fantasy. Thus scenarios for the future should never be thought of as final, or even irreversible; rather than regard them as blueprints for some distant destination, it would be better to see them simply as maps sketching possible routes out of a maze. First we must exit the labyrinth.

In this chapter, I start from the common socialist assumption that capitalism's central defects arise from the conflict between the pursuit of private profit and the satisfaction of human needs. I will then sketch out some of the considerations that would have to be taken into account in any attempt to remedy those defects.

What I'm not concerned with here is achieving some final and total harmony between the interests of each and the interests of all, or with cleansing humanity of conflict or egotism. I seek the *shortest* possible step from the society we have now to a society where most productive property is owned in common—not to rule out more radical change, but precisely to rule it in.

With the end of "actually existing socialism" after 1989, radicals responded in mainly two ways. Most stopped talking about a world after capitalism, retreating to a modest politics of piecemeal reform, or localism, or personal growth. The other response was exactly the opposite—an escape forward into the purest and most uncompromising visions of social reconstruction. In certain radical circles, this impulse involves a leap toward a world with no states or markets, and thus no money, wages, or prices: a system in which goods would be freely produced and freely taken, where the economy would be governed entirely by the maxim "from each according to ability, to each according to need."

Whenever such ideas are considered, debate seems to focus immediately on big philosophical questions about human nature. Skeptics scoff that people are too selfish for such a system to work. Optimists argue that humans are a naturally cooperative species. Evidence is adduced for both sides of the argument. But it's best to leave that debate to the side. It's safe to assume that humans display a mixture of cooperation and selfishness, in proportions that change according to circumstances.

The obstacles to a lofty vision of a stateless, marketless world are not so much moral as technical, and it's important to grasp exactly what they are.

We have to assume that we would not want to regress to some sharply lower stage of economic development; we would want to experience at least the same material comforts that we have under capitalism. On a *qualitative* level, of course, all sorts of things ought to change so that production better satisfies real human and ecological needs. But we would not want to see an overall decline in our productive powers.

But the kind of production of which we are now capable requires a vast and complex division of labor. This presents a tricky problem. To get a concrete sense of what it means, think of the way Americans lived at the time of the American Revolution, when the typical citizen worked on a small, relatively isolated family farm. Such households largely produced what they consumed and consumed what they produced. If they found themselves with a modest surplus of farm produce, they might sell it to others nearby, and with the money they earned they could buy a few luxuries. For the most part, though, they did not rely on other people to provide them with the things they needed to live.

Compare that situation with our own. Not only do we rely on others for our goods, but also the sheer *number* of people we rely on has increased to staggering proportions. Look around the room you're sitting in and think of your possessions. Now try to think of how many people were directly involved in their production. The laptop I'm typing on, for example, has a monitor, a case, a DVD player, and a microprocessor. Each was likely made in a separate factory, possibly in different countries, by various companies employing hundreds or thousands of workers. Then think of the raw plastic, metal, and rubber that went into those component parts, and all the people involved in producing them. Add the makers of the fuel that fired the factories and the ship crews and trucking fleets that got the computer to its destination. It's not hard to imagine millions of people participating in the production of just those items now sitting on my desk. And out of the millions of tasks involved, each individual performed only a tiny set of discrete steps.

How did they each know what to do? Of course, most of these people were employees, and their bosses told them what to do. But how did their bosses know how much plastic to produce? And how did they know to send the weaker, softer kind of plastic to the computer company, even though it would have been happy to take the sturdier, high-quality plastic reserved for the hospital equipment makers? And how did these manufacturers judge whether it was worth the extra resources to make laptops with nice LCD monitors, rather than being frugal and making older, simpler cathode ray models?

The total number of such dilemmas is practically infinite for a modern economy with millions of different products and billions of workers and consumers. And they must all be resolved in a way that is globally consistent, because at any given moment there are only so many workers and machines to go around, so making more of one thing means making less of another. Resources can be combined in an almost infinite number of possible permutations; some might satisfy society's material needs and desires fairly well, while others would be disastrous, involving huge quantities of unwanted production and lots of desirable things going unmade. In theory, any degree of success is possible.

This is the problem of economic calculation. In a market economy, prices perform this function. And the reason prices can work is that they convey systematic information concerning how much of one thing people are willing to give up to get another thing under a given set of circumstances. Only by requiring people to give up one thing to get another, in some ratio, can quantitative information be generated about how much, in relative terms, people value those things. And only by knowing how much relative value people place on millions of different things can producers embedded in this vast network make rational decisions about what their minute contribution to the overall system ought to be.

None of this means that calculation can be accomplished through prices alone, or that the prices generated in a market are somehow ideal or optimal. But there is no way a decentralized system could continually generate and broadcast so much quantitative information without the use of prices in some form. Of course, we don't have to have a decentralized system. We could have a centrally planned economy, in which all or most of society's production decisions are delegated to professional planners with computers. Their task would be extremely complex and their performance uncertain. But at least such a system would provide *some* method for economic calculation: the planners would try to gather all the necessary information into their central department and then figure out what everyone needs to do.

So *something* needs to perform the economic calculation function that prices do for a market system and planners do for a centrally planned system. As it happens, an attempt has been made to spell out exactly what would be required for economic calculation in a world with no states or markets. The anarchist activist Michael Albert and the economist Robin Hahnel have devised a system they call participatory economics, in which every individual's freely made decisions about production and consumption would be coordinated by means of a vast society-wide plan formulated through a "participatory" process with no central bureaucracy.

Parecon, as it's called, is an interesting exercise for our purposes because it rigorously works out exactly what would be needed to run such an "anarchist" economy. And the idea is roughly as follows: At the beginning of each year, everyone must write out a list of every item he or she plans to consume over the course of the year, along with the quantity of each item. In writing these lists, everyone consults a tentative list of prices for every product in the economy (keep in mind that there are more than two million products in Amazon.com's "kitchen and dining" category alone), and the total value of a person's requests may not exceed his or her personal "budget," which is determined by how much he or she promises to work that year.

Since the initial prices are only tentative estimates, a

network of direct-democratic councils must feed everyone's consumption lists and work pledges into computers to generate an improved set of prices that will bring planned levels of production and consumption (supply and demand) closer to balance. This improved price list is then published, which kicks off a second "iteration" of the process: now everyone has to rewrite their consumption requests and work pledges all over again, according to the new prices.

The whole procedure is repeated several times until supply and demand are finally balanced. Eventually everyone votes to choose among several possible plans.

In their speaking and writing, Albert and Hahnel narrate this remarkable process to show how attractive and feasible their system would be. But for many people—I would include myself in this group—the effect is exactly the opposite. It comes off instead as a precise demonstration of why economic calculation in the absence of markets or state planning would be, if perhaps not impossible in theory, at least impossible to imagine working in a way that most people could live with in practice. And parecon is itself a compromise from the purist's point of view, since it violates the principle "from each according to ability, to each according to need"—by limiting individuals' consumption requests to the extent of their work pledges. But of course without that stipulation, the plans wouldn't add up at all.

The point is not that a large-scale stateless, marketless economy simply wouldn't work. It's that, in the absence of some coordinating mechanism such as Albert and Hahnel's, it simply wouldn't exist in the first place. The problem of economic calculation, therefore, is something we have to take seriously if we want to contemplate something better than the status quo.

But what about the other alternative? Why not a centrally planned economy where the job of economic calculation is handed over to information-gathering experts—democratically accountable ones, it is hoped. We have historical examples of this kind of system, though of course they were far from democratic. Centrally planned economies registered some accomplishments: when communism came to poor, rural countries such as Bulgaria or Romania they were able to industrialize quickly, wipe out illiteracy, raise education levels, modernize gender roles, and eventually ensure that most people had basic housing and health care. The system could also raise per capita production pretty quickly from, say, the level of today's Laos to that of today's Bosnia; or from the level of Yemen to that of Egypt.

But beyond that, the system ran into trouble. Here a prefatory note is in order: because the neoliberal right has a habit of measuring a society's success by the abundance of its consumer goods, the radical left is prone to slip into a posture of denying this sort of thing is politically relevant at all. This is a mistake. The problem with full supermarket shelves is that they're not *enough*, not that they're unwelcome or trivial. The citizens of Communist countries experienced the paucity, shoddiness, and uniformity of their goods not merely as inconveniences; they experienced them as violations of their basic rights. As an anthropologist of Communist Hungary writes, "goods of state-socialist production . . . came to be seen as evidence of the failure of a state-socialist-generated modernity, but more importantly, of the regime's negligent and even 'inhumane' treatment of its subjects."

In fact, the shabbiness of consumer supply was popularly felt as a betrayal of the humanistic mission of socialism itself. An historian of East Germany quotes the petitions that ordinary consumers addressed to the state: "It really is not in the spirit of the human being as the center of socialist society when I have to save up for years for a Trabant and then cannot use my car for more than a year because of a shortage of spare parts!" said one. Another wrote, "When you read in the socialist press 'maximal satisfaction of the needs of the people and so on' and . . . 'everything for the benefit of the people,' it makes me feel sick." In different countries and languages across Eastern Europe, citizens used almost identical expressions to evoke the image of substandard goods being "thrown at" them.

Items that became unavailable in Hungary at various times due to planning failures included "the kitchen tool used to make Hungarian noodles," "bath plugs that fit tubs in stock"; "cosmetics shelves"; and "the metal box necessary for electrical wiring in new apartment buildings." As a local newspaper editorial complained in the 1960s, these things "don't seem important until the moment one needs them, and suddenly they are very important!"

And at an aggregate level, the best estimates showed the Communist countries steadily falling behind Western Europe: East German per capita income, which had been slightly higher than that of West German regions before World War II, never recovered in relative terms from the postwar occupation years and continually lost ground from 1960 onward. By the late 1980s it stood at less than 40 percent of the West German level. Unlike an imaginary economy with no states or markets, the Communist economies *did* have an economic calculation mechanism. It just didn't work as advertised.

What was the problem?

According to many Western economists, the answer was simple: the mechanism was too clumsy. In this telling, the problem had to do with the "invisible hand," the phrase Adam Smith had used only in passing but that later writers commandeered to reinterpret his insights about the role of prices, supply, and demand in allocating goods. Smith had originally invoked the price system to explain why market economies display a semblance of order at all, rather than chaos—why, for example, any desired commodity can usually be found conveniently for sale, even though there is no central authority seeing to its being produced.

But in the late nineteenth century, Smith's ideas were formalized by the founders of neoclassical economics, a tradition whose explanatory ambitions were far grander. They wrote equations representing buyers and sellers as vectors of supply and demand: when supply exceeded demand in a particular market, the price dropped; when demand exceeded supply, it rose. And when supply and demand were equal, the market in question was said to be in "equilibrium" and the price was said to be the "equilibrium price."

As for the economy as a whole, with its numberless, *interlocking* markets, it was not until 1954 that the future Nobel laureates Kenneth Arrow and Gérard Debreu made what was hailed as a momentous discovery in the theory of "general equilibrium"—a finding that, in the words of James Tobin, "lies at the very core of the scientific basis of economic theory." They proved mathematically that under specified assumptions, free markets were guaranteed to generate a set of potential equilibrium prices that could balance supply and demand in all markets *simultaneously*—and the resulting allocation of goods would be, in one important sense, "optimal": no one could be made better off without making someone else worse off.

The moral that could be extracted from this finding was that prices were not just a tool market economies used to create a degree of order and rationality. Rather, the prices that markets generated—*if* those markets were free and untrammeled—were optimal, and resulted in a maximally efficient allocation of resources. If the Communist system wasn't working, it was because the clumsy and fallible mechanism of planning couldn't arrive at this optimal solution.

This narrative resonated with the deepest instincts of the economics profession. The little just-so stories of economics textbooks explaining why minimum wages or rent controls ultimately make everyone worse off are meant to show that supply and demand dictate prices by a higher logic that mortals defy at their peril. These stories are "partial equilibrium" analyses—they only show what happens in an individual market artificially cut off from all the markets surrounding it. What Arrow and Debreu had supplied, the profession believed, was proof that this logic extends to the economy as a whole, with all its interlocking markets: a *general* equilibrium theory. In other words, it was proof that in the end, free-market prices will guide the economy as a whole to its optimum.

Thus, when Western economists descended on the former
Soviet bloc after 1989 to help direct the transition out of socialism, their central mantra, endlessly repeated, was "Get prices
right."

But a great deal of contrary evidence had accumulated in
the meantime. At about the time of the Soviet collapse, the
economist Peter Murrell published an article in the *Journal of
Economic Perspectives* reviewing empirical studies of efficiency
in the socialist planned economies. These studies consistently
failed to support the neoclassical analysis: virtually all of them
found that by standard neoclassical measures of efficiency,
the planned economies performed as well as or better than
market economies.

Murrell pleaded with readers to suspend their prejudices:

> The consistency and tenor of the results will surprise many
> readers. I was, and am, surprised at the nature of these
> results. And given their inconsistency with received doc-
> trines, there is a tendency to dismiss them on methodolog-
> ical grounds. However, such dismissal becomes increasingly
> hard when faced with a cumulation of consistent results
> from a variety of sources.

First he reviewed eighteen studies of technical efficiency:
the degree to which a firm produces at its own maximum
technological level. Matching studies of centrally planned
firms with studies that examined capitalist firms using the
same methodologies, he compared the results. One paper, for
example, found a 90 percent level of technical efficiency in
capitalist firms; another using the same method found a

93 percent level in Soviet firms. The results continued in the same way: 84 percent versus 86 percent, 87 percent versus 95 percent, and so on.

Then Murrell examined studies of allocative efficiency: the degree to which inputs are allocated among firms in a way that maximizes total output. One paper found that a fully optimal reallocation of inputs would increase total Soviet output by only 3 percent to 4 percent. Another found that raising Soviet efficiency to US standards would increase its GNP by all of 2 percent. A third produced a range of estimates as low as 1.5 percent. The highest number found in any of the Soviet studies was 10 percent. As Murrell notes, these were hardly amounts "likely to encourage the overthrow of a whole socio-economic system." (Murrell wasn't the only economist to notice this anomaly: an article titled "Why Is the Soviet Economy Allocatively Efficient?" appeared in *Soviet Studies* at about the same time.)

Two German micro economists tested the "widely accepted" hypothesis that "prices in a planned economy are arbitrarily set exchange ratios without any relation to relative scarcities or economic valuations [whereas] capitalist market prices are close to equilibrium levels." They employed a technique that analyzes the distribution of an economy's inputs among industries to measure how far the pattern diverges from what would be expected to prevail under perfectly optimal neoclassical prices. Examining East German and West German data from 1987, they arrived at an "astonishing result": the divergence was 16.1 percent in the West and 16.5 percent in the East, a trivial difference. The gap in the West's favor, they wrote, was greatest in the manufacturing sectors, where something like competitive conditions may have existed. But in the bulk of the West German economy—which was then being hailed globally as *Modell Deutschland*—monopolies, taxes, subsidies, and so on actually left its price structure *farther* from the "efficient" optimum than in the moribund Communist system behind the Berlin Wall.

The neoclassical model also seemed belied by the largely failed experiments with more marketized versions of socialism in Eastern Europe. Beginning in the mid-1950s, reformist economists and intellectuals in the region had been pushing for the introduction of market mechanisms to rationalize production. Reforms were attempted in a number of countries with varying degrees of seriousness, including in the abortive Prague Spring. But the country that went farthest in this direction was Hungary, which inaugurated its "new economic mechanism" in 1968. Firms were still owned by the state, but now they were expected to buy and sell on the open market and maximize profits. The results were disappointing. Although in the 1970s Hungary's looser consumer economy earned it the foreign correspondent's cliché "the happiest barracks in the Soviet bloc," its dismal productivity growth did not improve and shortages were still common.

If all these facts and findings represented one reason to doubt the neoclassical narrative, there was a more fundamental reason: economists had discovered gaping holes in the theory itself. In the years since Arrow and Debreu had drafted their famous proof that free markets under the right conditions could generate optimal prices, theorists (including

Debreu himself) had uncovered some disturbing features of the model. It turned out that such hypothetical economies generated *multiple* sets of possible equilibrium prices, and there was no mechanism to ensure that the economy would settle on any one of them without long or possibly endless cycles of chaotic trial and error. Even worse, the model's results couldn't withstand much relaxation of its patently unrealistic initial assumptions; for example, without perfectly competitive markets—which are virtually nonexistent in the real world—there was no reason to expect any equilibrium at all.

Even the liberal trope that government interventions are justified by "market failures"—specific anomalies that depart from the Arrow-Debreu model's perfect-market assumptions—was undermined by another finding of the 1950s: the "general theory of the second best." Introduced by Richard Lipsey and Kelvin Lancaster, the theorem proves that even if the idealized assumptions of the standard model are accepted, attempts to correct "market failures" and "distortions" (such as tariffs, price controls, monopolies, or externalities) are as likely to make things worse as to make them better, as long as any other market failures remain uncorrected—which will always be the case in a world of endemic imperfect competition and limited information.

In a wide-ranging review of "the failure of general equilibrium theory," the economist Frank Ackerman[1] concluded:

A story about Adam Smith, the invisible hand, and the merits of markets pervades introductory textbooks, classroom teaching, and contemporary political discourse. The intellectual foundation of this story rests on general equilibrium. . . . If the foundation of everyone's favorite economics story is now known to be unsound . . . then the profession owes the world a bit of an explanation.

The point is this: if a deterministic story about free markets generating optimal prices leading to maximum output was no longer viable, then the failure of planned economies could hardly be attributed to the absence of those features. As Communist systems were collapsing in Eastern Europe, economists who had lost faith in the neoclassical narrative began to argue that an alternative explanation was needed. The most prominent theorist in this group was Joseph Stiglitz, who had become famous for his work on the economics of information. His arguments dovetailed with those of other dissenters from the neoclassical approach, such as the eminent Hungarian scholar of planned economies János Kornai and evolutionary economists such as Peter Murrell. They all pointed to a number of characteristics, largely ignored by the neoclassical school, that better accounted for the ability of market economies to avoid the problems plaguing centrally planned systems. The aspects they emphasized were disparate, but they all tended to arise from a single, rather simple fact: in market systems *firms are autonomous.*

That means that within the limits of the law, a firm may enter a market; choose its products and production methods; interact with other firms and individuals; and must close down if it cannot get by on its own resources. As a textbook on central planning put it, in market systems the presumption is "that an activity may be undertaken unless it is expressly prohibited," whereas in planned systems "the prevailing presumption in most areas of economic life is that an activity *may not* be undertaken unless permission has been obtained from the appropriate authority." The neoclassical fixation with ensuring that firms exercised this autonomy in a laissez-faire environment—that restrictions on voluntary exchange be minimized or eliminated—was essentially beside the point.

Thus, free entry and multiple autonomous sources of capital mean that anyone with novel production ideas can seek resources to implement their ideas and doesn't face a single veto point within a planning apparatus. As a result, they stand a much greater chance of obtaining the resources to test out their ideas. This probably leads to more of the waste inherent in failed experiments—but also far greater scope for improved products and processes, and a constantly higher rate of technological improvement and productivity growth.

Firms' autonomy to choose their products and production methods means they can communicate directly with customers and tailor their output to their needs—and with free entry customers can choose among the output of different producers: no agency needs to spell out what needs to be produced. To illustrate the relative informational efficiency of this kind of system, Stiglitz cited a Defense Department contract for the production of plain white T-shirts: in the tender for bidding, the physical description of the T-shirt desired ran to thirty small-print pages. In other words, a centralized agency could never learn and then specify every desired characteristic of every product.

Meanwhile, East European economists realized that an essential precondition for firms to be truly autonomous was the existence of a *capital market*—and this helped explain the failure of Hungary's market-oriented reforms. In seeking an explanation for the persistence of shortages under the new market system, the Hungarian economist János Kornai had identified a phenomenon he called the "soft budget constraint"—a situation where the state continually transfers resources to loss-making firms to prevent them from failing. This phenomenon, he argued, was what lay behind the shortage problem in Hungary: expecting that they would always be prevented from going bankrupt, firms operated in practice without a budget constraint and thus exerted limitless demand for materials and capital goods, causing chronic production bottlenecks.

But why did the state keep bailing out the troubled firms? It's not as if the Hungarian authorities were opposed to firm failures on principle. In fact, when bankruptcies did happen, the Communist leadership treated them as public relations events, to demonstrate their commitment to a rational economic system.

The ultimate answer was the absence of a capital market. In a market economy, a troubled firm can sell part or all of its operations to another firm. Or it can seek capital from lenders or investors, if it can convince them it has the potential to improve its performance. But in the absence of a capital market, the only practical options are bankruptcy or bailouts. Constant bailouts were the price the Hungarian leadership was forced to pay to avoid extremely high and wasteful rates of firm failures. In other words, capital markets provide a rational way to deal with the turbulence caused by the hard budget constraints of market systems: when a firm needs to spend more than its income, it can turn to lenders and investors. Without a capital market, that option is foreclosed.

As resistance against communism rose, those in Eastern Europe who wished to avoid a turn to capitalism drew the appropriate lessons. In 1989, the dissident Polish reform economists Włodzimierz Brus and Kazimierz Łaski—both convinced socialists and disciples of the distinguished Marxist-Keynesian Michał Kalecki—published a book examining the prospects for East European reform. Both had been influential proponents of democratic reforms and socialist market mechanisms since the 1950s.

Their conclusion now was that to have a rational market socialism, publicly owned firms would have to be made autonomous—and this would require a *socialized capital market*. The authors made it clear that this would entail a fundamental reordering of the political economy of East European systems—and indeed of traditional notions of socialism. Writing on the eve of the upheavals that would bring down communism, they set out their vision: "the role of the owner-state should be separated from the state as an authority in charge of administration. . . . [E]nterprises . . . have to become separated not only from the state in its wider role but also from each other."

The vision Brus and Łaski sketched was novel: a constellation of autonomous firms, financed by a multiplicity of autonomous banks or investment funds, all competing and interacting in a market—yet all nevertheless socially owned.

All of this lays the groundwork for raising the critical

question of *profit*. There are two ways to think about the function of profits under capitalism. In the Marxist conception, capitalists' restless search for profit drives the pace and shape of economic growth, making it the ultimate "motor of the system"—but it's judged to be an erratic and arbitrary motor that ought to be replaced by something more rational and humane. In mainstream economics, on the other hand, profits are understood simply as a benign coordinating signal, broadcasting information to firms and entrepreneurs about how to satisfy society's needs most efficiently.

Each of these versions contains some truth. Look at the mainstream account. Its logic is straightforward: a firm's profit is the market value of the output it sells minus the market value of the inputs it buys. So the pursuit of profit leads firms to maximize their production of socially desired outputs while economizing on their use of scarce inputs. On this logic, profits are an ideal coordinating device.

But the logic holds only to the extent that an item's market value is actually a good measure of its social value. Does that assumption hold? Leftists know enough to scoff at that idea. The history of capitalism is a compendium of misvalued goods. Not only do capitalists draw from a treasury of tricks and maneuvers to inflate the market value of the outputs they sell (for example, through advertising) and drive down the value of the inputs they have to buy (for example, by de-skilling labor), but also capitalism itself systematically produces prices for crucial goods that bear little rational relation to their marginal social value: just think of health insurance, natural resources, interest rates, wages.

So if profit is a signal, it invariably comes mixed with a lot of noise. Still, there's an important signal there. Most of the millions of goods in the economy aren't like health insurance or natural resources; they're more banal—such as rubber bands, sheet metal, or flat-screen TVs. The relative prices of these goods do seem to function as decent guides to their relative marginal social values. When it comes to *this* portion of firms' inputs and outputs—say, a steel company that buys iron and sells it manufactured as steel—profit-seeking really does make capitalists want to produce in the most efficient way possible things people desire. It's those crucial misvalued goods—labor, nature, information, finance, risk, and so on—that produce the irrationality of profit.

In other words, under capitalism firms *can* increase their profits by efficiently producing things people want. But they can also increase them by immiserating their workers, despoiling the environment, defrauding consumers, or indebting the populace. How do you obtain one without getting the other?

The standard answer to this dilemma is what you might call the social democratic solution: let firms pursue their private profits, but have the state intervene case by case to forbid them from doing so in socially harmful ways. Ban pollution, give rights to workers, forbid consumer fraud, and repress speculation. This agenda is nothing to sneeze at. The social theorist Karl Polanyi saw it as part of what he called the long "double movement" that had been under way ever since the industrial revolution. Polanyi argued that liberal capitalism had always been pushed forward by a drive to turn everything into a commodity. Because it required that production be "organized through a self-regulating mechanism of barter and exchange," it demanded that "man and nature must be brought into its orbit; they must be subject to supply and demand, that is, be dealt with as commodities, as goods produced for sale."

But that commodifying drive had always produced its dialectical opposite, a countermovement from society below, seeking decommodification. Thus Polanyi's double movement was "the action of two organizing principles in society, each of them setting itself specific institutional aims, having the support of definite social forces and using its own distinctive methods":

> The one was the principle of economic liberalism, aiming at the establishment of a self-regulating market, relying on the support of the trading classes, and using largely laissez-faire and free trade as its methods; the other was the principle of social protection aiming at the conservation of man and nature as well as productive organization, relying on the varying support of those most immediately affected by the deleterious action of the market—primarily, but not exclusively, the working and the landed classes—and using protective legislation, restrictive associations, and other instruments of intervention as its methods.

After the Second World War, the pressure of the countermovement made decommodification the unacknowledged motor of domestic politics throughout the industrialized world. Parties of the working class, acutely vulnerable to pressure from below, were in government more than 40 percent of the time in the postwar decades—compared to about

10 percent in the interwar years, and almost never before that—and "contagion from the left" forced parties of the right into defensive acquiescence. Schooling, medical treatment, housing, retirement, leisure, child care, subsistence itself, but most importantly, wage-labor: these were to be gradually removed from the sphere of market pressure, transformed from goods requiring money, or articles bought and sold on the basis of supply and demand, into social rights and objects of democratic decision.

This, at least, was the maximal social-democratic program—and in certain times and places in the postwar era its achievements were dramatic.

But the social democratic solution is unstable—and this is where the Marxist conception comes in, with its stress on pursuit of profit as the motor of the capitalist system. There's a fundamental contradiction between accepting that capitalists' pursuit of profit will be the *motor* of the system, and believing you can systematically tame and repress it through policies and regulations. In the classical Marxist account, the contradiction is straightforwardly economic: policies that reduce profit rates too much will lead to underinvestment and economic crisis. But the contradiction can also be political: profit-hungry capitalists will use their social power to obstruct the necessary policies. How can you have a system *driven* by individuals maximizing their profit cash flows and still expect to maintain the profit-repressing norms, rules, laws, and regulations necessary to uphold the common welfare?

What is needed is a structure that allows autonomous firms to produce and trade goods for the market, aiming to generate a surplus of output over input—while keeping those firms public and preventing their surplus from being appropriated by a narrow class of capitalists. Under this type of system, workers can assume any degree of control they like over the management of their firms, and any "profits" can be socialized—that is, they can truly function as a signal rather than as a motive force. But the precondition of such a system is the socialization of the means of production—structured in a way that preserves the existence of a capital market. How can all this be done?

Start with the basics. Private control over society's productive infrastructure is ultimately a financial phenomenon. It is by financing the means of production that capitalists exercise control, as a class or as individuals. What's needed, then, is a *socialization of finance*—that is, a system of common, collective financing of the means of production and credit. But what does that mean in practice?

It might be said that people own two kinds of assets. "Personal" assets include houses, cars, or computers. But financial assets—claims on money flows such as stocks, bonds, and mutual funds—are what finance the productive infrastructure. Suppose a public common fund were established to undertake what might be euphemistically called the "compulsory purchase" of all privately owned financial assets. It would, for example, "buy" a person's mutual fund shares at their market price, depositing payment in the person's bank account. By the end of this process, the common fund would own all formerly privately owned financial assets, while all the financial wealth of individuals would be converted into bank deposits (but with the banks in question now owned in common, since the common fund now owns all the shares).

No one has lost any wealth; they've simply cashed out their stocks and bonds. But there are far-reaching consequences. Society's means of production and credit now constitute the assets of a public fund, while individuals' financial wealth balances are now its liabilities. In other words, the job of intermediating between individuals' money savings and society's productive physical assets that used to be performed by capitalist banks, mutual funds, and so on, has been socialized. The common fund can now reestablish a "tamed" capital market on a socialized basis, with a multiplicity of socialized banks and investment funds owning and allocating capital among the means of production.

The lesson here is that the transformation to a different system does not have to be catastrophic. Of course, the situation I'm describing would be a revolutionary one—but it wouldn't have to involve the total collapse of the old society and the Promethean conjuring of something entirely unrecognizable in its place.

At the end of the process, firms no longer have individual owners who seek to maximize profits. Instead, they are owned by society as a whole, along with any surplus ("profits") they might generate. Since firms still buy and sell in the market, they can still generate a surplus (or deficit) that can be used to judge their efficacy. But no individual owner actually pockets these surpluses, meaning that no one has any particular interest in perpetuating or exploiting the profit-driven misvaluation of goods that is endemic under capitalism. The "social democratic solution" that was once a contradiction—

selectively frustrating the profit motive to uphold the common good while systematically relying on it as the engine of the system—can now be reconciled.

To the same end, the accrual of interest to individuals' bank deposits can be capped at a certain threshold of wealth, and beyond that level it could be limited to simply compensate for inflation. (Or the social surplus could be divided up equally among everyone and just paid out as a social dividend.) This would yield not exactly the euthanasia of the rentier, but of the rentier "interest" in society. And while individuals could still be free to start businesses, once their firms reached a certain size, age, and importance, they would have to "go public": to be sold by their owners into the socialized capital market.

What I'm describing is, in one sense, the culmination of a trend that has been proceeding under capitalism for centuries: the growing separation of ownership from control. Already in the mid-nineteenth century, Marx marveled at the proliferation of what we now call corporations: "Stock companies in general—developed with the credit system—have an increasing tendency to separate this work of management as a function from the ownership of capital, be it self-owned or borrowed. Just as the development of bourgeois society witnessed a separation of the functions of judges and administrators from land-ownership, whose attributes they were in feudal times." Marx thought this development highly significant: "It is the abolition of capital as private property within the framework of capitalist production itself."

By the 1930s this "socialized private property" had become the dominant productive form in American capitalism, as

Adolf Berle and Gardiner Means signaled in *The Modern Corporation and Private Property*. The managerial-corporate model seemed to face a challenge in the 1980s when capitalist owners, dissatisfied with languishing profit rates, launched an offensive against what they saw as lax and complacent corporate managers. This set off a titanic intraclass brawl for control of the corporation that lasted more than a decade. But by the late 1990s, the result was a self-serving compromise on both sides: CEOs retained their autonomy from the capital markets, but embraced the ideology of "shareholder value"; their stock packages were made more sensitive to the firm's profit and stock-market performance, but also massively inflated. In reality, none of this technically resolved the problem of the separation of ownership and control, since the new pay schemes never came close to really aligning the pecuniary interests of the managers with the owners'. A comprehensive study of executive pay from 1936 to 2005 by MIT and Federal Reserve economists found that the correlation between firms' performance and their executives' total pay was negligible—not only in the era of midcentury managerialism, but throughout the whole period.

In other words, the laboratory of capitalism has been pursuing a centuries-long experiment to test whether an economic system can function when it severs the one-to-one link between the profits of an enterprise and the rewards that accrue to its controllers. The experiment has been a success. Contemporary capitalism, with its quite radical separation of ownership and control, has no shortage of defects and pathologies, but an inattention to profit has not been one of them.

How should these socialized firms actually be governed? A complete answer to that question lies far beyond the scope of a chapter like this; minutely describing the charters and bylaws of imaginary enterprises is exactly the kind of "cook-shop" recipe that Marx rightly ridiculed. But the basic point is clear enough: since these firms buy and sell in the market, their performance can be rationally judged. A firm could be controlled entirely by its workers, in which case they could simply collect its entire net income after paying for the use of the capital.[2] Or it could be "owned" by an entity in the social-ized capital market, with a management selected by that entity and a strong system of worker codetermination to counterbal-ance it within the firm. Those managers and "owners" could be evaluated on the *relative* returns the firm generates, but they would have no private property rights over the *absolute* mass of profits.[3] If expectations of future performance needed to be "objectively" judged in some way, that is some-thing the socialized capital markets could do.

Such a program does not amount to a utopia; it does not proclaim Year Zero or treat society as a blank slate. What it tries to do is sketch a rational economic mechanism that denies the pursuit of profit priority over the fulfillment of human needs. Nor does it rule out further, more basic changes in the way humans interact with each other and their environment; on the contrary, it lowers the barriers to further change.

In a tribute to Isaac Deutscher, the historian Ellen Meiksins-Wood praised his "measured vision of socialism, which recognized its promise for human emancipation without harboring romantic illusions that it would cure all human ills,

CODA

Peter Frase and Bhaskar Sunkara

You get what you pay for, and we haven't paid for much.

Compared to other rich countries, the United States does little to ensure its citizens have access to vital services or to prevent them from falling into deprivation due to unemployment or low-wage labor. At 19.4 percent of GDP, American social spending is far below the 25 to 30 percent budgeted in most of Western Europe. Meanwhile, 16 percent of Americans lack health insurance, almost a quarter of our children live in poverty, and millions are unemployed.

Yet not only does an expansion of the safety net seem politically impossible, even existing protections are under attack everywhere. But a movement to extend social protections has the potential to foster a new majoritarian left coalition.

Republicans know this—that's why they manipulate the way welfare is perceived at every turn.

The reality is that 96 percent of Americans have benefited from government programs, but the right works hard to hide that fact. It's part of a deliberate strategy to divide the country into two camps by convincing the majority of voters that their labor is benefiting parasites dependent on the social safety net.

Democrats have too often bolstered this effort by echoing calls for "welfare reform" and "fiscal responsibility" and by supporting policies that channel benefits through the tax code (such as the home-mortgage deduction) and private organizations (such as employer-provided health insurance). The result is a system that provides few benefits, makes them largely invisible, and disproportionately serves the more affluent.

In the face of this neoliberal consensus, the left's counter-mission must be to show that social democracy benefits everyone. The efforts of generations of liberals have rarely gone beyond rebranding and messaging. Few have pushed for the structural changes necessary to build a strong welfare state.

Given the country's economic situation and the massive discontent at the political level, the left is in the best position in decades to argue for social-democratic programs. Austerity has only worsened unemployment and stagnated wages, and only a concerted effort to create jobs and boost purchasing power can revive growth and restore employment. Despite fear-mongering about the effects of budget deficits, the government is still able to borrow money virtually interest-free.

And contrary to right-wing claims of out-of-control spending, taxes as a percentage of GDP are at their lowest level since 1950. We can and should ensure that everyone has access to health care, education, a secure retirement, and a livable income regardless of labor market uncertainties.

Most on the left would agree with these goals; the question has always been how to achieve them.

We think we have an answer. We propose a new anti-austerity coalition united by the immediate demand that certain social spending burdens, currently borne by states and municipalities, be federalized. Almost all states are legally required to keep balanced budgets, making it unfeasible for them to deploy deficit spending. Even if these laws were changed, states would still face greater difficulties in this arena than the federal government. States could never borrow money on as favorable terms as the United States can, and they haven't been printing their own currencies since the Articles of Confederation.

Simply put, without centralization, social democracy in America is impossible. Once achieved, progressives could pursue policies that not only immediately improve working-class lives, but also lay the groundwork for more radical reforms in the future. Which is to say that the left needs an affirmative strategy that can go beyond the piecemeal defense of the status quo against austerity. We need a comprehensive strategy that is adapted to the current state of our politics and economy and that draws on existing areas of progressive strength.

For too long, liberals have focused on technocratic policy analyses, seeking granular remedies to isolated problems.

Such solutions lack the kind of sweeping political vision that wins and sustains policy reforms. Conversely, radicals have for too long made rhetorical appeals without any grounding in political realities. The plan outlined here is a corrective to both trends, written with the understanding that wonky policy and class politics are inextricably linked.

Though the struggle over state budget cuts has sparked debate at the national level, the politics of austerity has been prominent in the lower levels of government. Indeed, as long as social welfare programs are funded at the state and local levels, the fiscal limitations of subnational governments make expanding the safety net nearly impossible in the future. Local movements may sporadically succeed at funding sporadic programs, but they will be fighting a losing battle as long as they are trying to win concessions from governments with little spending flexibility. In the long run, building a better and more robust social safety net will mean unifying and reorganizing our fragmented welfare state. Some liberals defend the current system by holding up the states as "laboratories of democracy" that can pioneer new progressive initiatives that are impossible at the national level. Historically, however, the least progressive aspects of American welfare have been those that are passed off to the states, while the most generous and universal are national programs.

As the political scientist Suzanne Mettler observes in her book *Dividing Citizens: Gender and Federalism in New Deal Public Policy*, the elements of the New Deal that were left to the states were largely those that serve women and minori-

ties, and these programs tend to subject recipients to surveillance and scrutiny by bureaucrats and social workers. National
programs such as Social Security and Medicare, which have
a large proportion of white men on their rolls, are by contrast regarded as entitlements and their recipients treated
with respect.

This pattern is likely to be perpetuated, especially by right-
leaning states that are both hostile to welfare programs and
contain a disproportionate share of the nation's poor. It's no
coincidence that Mitt Romney and Paul Ryan's 2012 budget
plan planned to push even more social welfare administration
onto the states, by converting programs such as Medicaid and
food stamps into block grants.

Given the current disarray, a one-size-fits-all solution for
consolidating the welfare state does not exist. Under a new
progressive system, state and local spending could be trans-
ferred to federal programs in various ways.

WELFARE AND UNEMPLOYMENT

In these cases, where benefits are already a shared responsibility of federal and nonfederal governments, Washington
must simply assume more of the responsibility.

PENSIONS

The current shortfall in pension funds is largely a result of the
2008 stock-market collapse after the burst of the housing bubble, a circumstantial, not essential, deprivation of funds. But
some type of federal guarantee for these plans is required to

ensure that workers receive the benefits they are contractu-
ally entitled to, especially in times of recession.

The federal government already has an entity, the Pension
Benefit Guaranty Corporation, responsible for ensuring that
private-sector employees receive their pensions even when
their plans fail or their employers go bankrupt. Something
analogous could be created for employees of local and state
governments. As a long-term solution, however, it makes little
sense for state and local public-sector pensions to be on local
budgets and subject to the fluctuations of the stock market.
These workers should be fully brought into the Social Security
system, like their private-sector and federal counterparts.

HEALTH CARE

Alleviating the burden of health care spending on the states
will require addressing the irrationalities of the American
health-care system, which is far more expensive than systems
of comparable quality in other countries. The Affordable Care
Act made incremental progress in this direction, but something like a national single-payer system is necessary to relieve
cost pressures on both the states and the federal government.
A first step along that road would be to make Medicaid a fully
federally run program, analogous to Medicare.

EDUCATION

Because education is the most localized category of social
spending, it will be the most difficult to address. But because

it makes up the largest component of nonfederal spending, not to mention its role at the forefront of corporate reform efforts, it is also the most important.

In the near term, demanding infusions of federal support for local education could go a long way toward equalizing access to education. In the long run, we should not lose sight of the inequality that inevitably results from allowing schools to be funded and administrated locally, nor should we take that localism as a necessity. In the past, the Supreme Court has held that education is not a fundamental right, and therefore a system of unequal K–12 school systems funded by local property taxes is constitutional. But our fragmented and unequal educational system is a strange and inferior institution compared to what exists in other rich countries.

These commonsense fixes have long been out of reach. And yet, though the left has been in retreat since the 1960s, there are new signs of life. The new coalition will be cobbled together from outgrowths of new protest movements, like Occupy Wall Street and Black Lives Matter, and more recent labor insurgencies. We propose that protest-oriented movements, militant sectors in the labor movement, and left-wing elected officials at the state and local levels could form a motley and potentially powerful antiausterity coalition.

A broader shift to the left among Americans under thirty has already begun, reflecting the frustration of young people facing rising inequality and diminishing economic prospects.

The recession hit this demographic group especially hard, and its effects will dog them throughout their lives. Those who have entered the job market in recent years face lower employment rates, worse wages, and higher debts than those who preceded them.

The Occupy movement left the streets some years ago. It did, however, unleash a wave of politicization that remains with us. Thousands of people are still active in groups that found their genesis in Occupy. Moreover, the idea that elites use their wealth and power to the detriment of the vast majority of people has introduced a level of class analysis into the national public debate unseen in eighty years.

The early success of Occupy owed much to a creative wellspring from the anarchist movement. The novel idea of occupying space and creating camps is testimony to that. But too many within the movement saw those encampments as models of a future postcapitalist utopia, rather than merely tactical deployments. Not surprisingly, they failed to connect these tactics to a wider political strategy.

Occupy's failure in this respect and its inability to translate its energy into more sustained organizing around a broad anti-austerity message reflect both historical—and innate—weaknesses within the anarchist movement and activists' fears of being co-opted into a neoliberal electoral framework.

By linking younger activists on the extraparliamentary left with labor unions and policymakers under an umbrella program that's both radical and achievable, Occupy activists could contribute to tangible progressive change without sacrificing their uncompromising zeal.

ORGANIZED LABOR

Today, only 12 percent of the workforce belongs to labor unions. However, 37 percent of public employees are unionized, compared to just 7 percent in the private sector. This is both a striking sign of the American left's decline and a reason why resistance to the current economic crisis has been hard to muster.

That the public sector houses what remains of the labor movement is taken by many to be an indication of the movement's terminal decline. And even this last union bastion is eroding.

Cash-strapped states and cities have launched an effective bipartisan attack on the salaries, benefits, and collective bargaining rights of public workers. Scott Walker's victory against collective organizing in Wisconsin was just the most outrageous example of a generalized phenomenon. In the context of local competition over resources and general economic downturn, public employees are easy targets.

The strength of a middle-class politics built around resentment should not be underestimated: Walker had a real social base, and thousands were energized around antiunion sentiment. His supporters saw union pensions, health benefits, and worker protections as special privileges stolen from more productive sectors in the private economy, rather than as the just rewards for hard labor that everyone deserves. Even some liberals, sympathetic to unions in the private sector, view the interests of unionized public employees and the interests of the public they serve as at odds.

Instead of asking "Why not me?" this anti-working-class alliance demands "Why them?" For this precise reason, shifting fiscal burdens from underwater state and local budgets onto firmer, federal terrain is vital. But in the meantime, we should accept that the labor movement is now concentrated in the public sector. This can be turned into a source of strength.

Some see public-sector unions as little more than cartels that protect the privileges and pay of their members. But these unions can be the chief protectors of big federal programs. And if the public sector were more stable, with its jobs linked to politically untouchable and universal federal programs, public-sector unions could have clout similar to that of their powerful European counterparts, visible and reliable protectors of the welfare state.

Historically, public-sector unions are more oriented than their private-sector counterparts toward a social-movement unionism—connecting organically with their communities rather than limiting their struggles to shop-floor-level disputes. This broader orientation was critical to the mass local support the Chicago Teachers' Union garnered in its struggle in the fall of 2012 against Mayor Rahm Emanuel's assault on their bargaining rights and compensation. By devoting significant resources toward community outreach and tying its demands to a vision of egalitarian public education, the union made the strike about more than just wages and benefits.

Creating a new set of union proxies, either directly or by engagement with outside radical social movements, could also drive this coalition against austerity. These organizations could circumvent restrictive labor laws and build alliances with both nonunion workers and the unemployed. Actions pitched at this community level can show the public that unions are more than self-interested actors and make labor a cornerstone of a broader progressive movement.

The labor movement also has the ability to connect the outsider power of protest with the insider business of writing and lobbying for legislation. Unions have both the resources and the experience to sway Washington. This will be a necessity for any movement that seeks to reshape the structure of the American welfare state, an important complement to the visibility and disruptive potential of street protest.

Local and state officials will be necessary collaborators. Our strategy would generate political pressure first and most intensely at the state and local levels. Local governments' drive toward austerity has much to do with their intense budget constraints.

Our era lacks the robust urban political coalitions that characterized the period when left-wing social scientists Richard Cloward and Frances Fox Piven suggested banding together to overwhelm the welfare rolls, proving the inadequacy of the American welfare state to meet basic needs. At that time, the civil rights movement was able to forge alliances between urban people of color and affluent, educated white liberals—and often against working-class political machines that excluded nonwhites.

Today, however, elite liberals are arrayed against what they regard as the modern machine: a "bloated" public sector that has become one of the few sources of stable, middle-class jobs for people of color. Neoliberal leaders such as New York's former mayor Michael Bloomberg and Chicago's Rahm Emanuel unapologetically represent the interests of wealthy business owners against the working class, pushing austerity and privatization as the solutions to fiscal crises. Breaking the power of this political bloc will necessitate offering fiscally stressed governors and mayors an alternative path.

State and local officials are generally happy to have the burden of social spending taken off their hands, whatever their nominal ideological commitments. The right may have denounced Obama's stimulus bill, but most Republican governors and mayors didn't turn down the money.

If progressives can articulate a positive political vision while simultaneously pushing for policies to ease the fiscal burden on states and cities, they will offer voters and officials an alternative that is appealing and practical. While refusing to sacrifice public services or jobs on the altar of balanced budgets, the left could ally with state and local leaders to lobby for national solutions to fiscal crises.

THE FUTURE WE WANT

The left must not only defeat austerity and preserve the social safety net; it must do so in a way that assembles the forces necessary for more fundamental transformations in the future.

This vision should be premeditated. We can't go back to the postwar Golden Age of the American welfare state, but we can build a system in the twenty-first century that embodies what people remember most from that era—an overriding sense of freedom. Freedom to give their children an education without rival. Freedom from poverty, hunger, and homelessness. Freedom to grow into old age with pensions, Social Security, and affordable and accessible health care. Freedom to leave an exploitative work environment and find another job. Freedom to organize with fellow workers for redress.

The appeal of such a society, combined with the political strategy needed to make it a reality, will pave the way for the institution of a new set of economic and social rights to complement our bedrock political and civil rights. These steps are necessary to build the type of working-class power that can in time win more radical transformations.

What kind of society would we build? Russian revolutionary Leon Trotsky's belief that if nourished the average person could rise to the heights of an Aristotle, Goethe, or Marx is perhaps too ambitious. But we can imagine a better future, one where technology makes the pace of work more and not less tolerable, where democracy is radically expanded into our workplaces and our homes, where competition and exploitation eventually become barely remembered relics of an inhumane age.

NOTES

IMAGINING SOCIALIST EDUCATION

1. Melissa Stanger, "The 50 Most Expensive Private High Schools in America," *Business Insider*, October 1, 2014, http://www .businessinsider.com/most-expensive-private-schools-in-the-us -2014-8#.
2. U.S. Census Bureau, "Median and Average Sales Prices of New Homes Sold in United States: Annual Data," http://www.census .gov/const/uspriceann.pdf.
3. The Rudolf Steiner School, New York City, http://steiner.edu /tuition/.
4. Amazon founder Jeff Bezos attended a Montessori preschool, an educational model that, like Avenues, is built around curriculum and instruction that promotes learning through discovery and respect for the learner. The inventor of the Sims video games has said, "SimCity comes right out of Montessori."

5. *Wired* magazine calls student-centered learning "a decidedly Bay Area experiment"; Issie Lapowsky, "Inside the School Silicon Valley Thinks Will Save Education," *Wired*, May 4, 2015, http://www.wired.com/2015/05/altschool/.

6. "Back to School Basics," National Center for Education Statistics, http://nces.ed.gov/fastfacts/display.asp?id=372.

7. Catherine Gewertz, "Study: Districts Vary Widely in the Amount of Time They Spend on Testing," *Education Week*, February 5, 2014, http://blogs.edweek.org/edweek/curriculum/2014/02/time_spent_on_student_testing.html.

8. For a deep discussion of this complex issue, see Annette Lareau's *Unequal Childhoods: Class, Race, and Family Life* (2003).

9. Gary Orfield and Chungmei Lee, *Why Segregation Matters: Poverty and Educational Inequality* (Cambridge, Mass.: Civil Rights Project, Harvard University, 2005); Richard Fry, and Paul Taylor, "The Rise of Residential Segregation by Income," Pewsocialtrends .org. August 1, 2012. Web.

10. David C. Berliner and Bruce J. Biddle, "What Research Says About Unequal Funding for Schools in America," Education Policy Reports Project, Arizona State University, 2012.

11. Jenny Brundin, "Thousands of Students Protest Colorado Standardized Tests," Colorado Public Radio, November 13, 2014, http://www.cpr.org/news/story/thousands-students-protest -colorado-standardized-tests.

12. Chris McKee and Lysee Mitri, "Standing Up to Standardized Tests: Hundreds of Students Walk Out in New Mexico," WKBN, March 3, 2015, http://wkbn.com/2015/03/03/standing-up-to -standardized-tests-hundreds-of-students-walk-out/; http://www .theguardian.com/education/2015/mar/02/new-mexico-high -school-students-walkout-protest-common-core-testing.

13. Eric M. Johnson, "Seattle High School Junior Class Skips Standardized Test in Protest," Reuters, April 24, 2015, http://www .reuters.com/article/2015/04/24/us-usa-education-washington -idUSKBN0NF22920150424.

14. Anya Kamenetz, "Anti-Test 'Opt-Out' Movement Makes a Wave in New York State," NPR, April 20, 2015, http://www.npr.org /blogs/ed/2015/04/20/400396254/anti-test-opt-out-movement -makes-a-wave-in-new-york-state.

THE CURE FOR BAD SCIENCE

1. Will Wilkinson, "Barbara Fredrickson's Bestselling *Positivity* Is Trashed by a New Study," *Daily Beast*, August 16, 2013, http:// www.thedailybeast.com/articles/2013/08/16/barbara -fredrickson-s-bestselling-positivity-is-trashed-by-a-new-study .html.

2. "Metaphysicians," *Economist*, March 15, 2014, http://www .economist.com/news/science-and-technology/21598944-sloppy -researchers-beware-new-institute-has-you-its-sights -metaphysicians.

FINDING THE FUTURE OF CRIMINAL JUSTICE

1. An initiative established by President Barack Obama to "reduce disparities and enhance positive outcomes for all youth, including boys and young men of color."

2. The white Ferguson, Missouri, police officer who shot and killed Michael Brown, an unarmed eighteen-year-old black man, in August 2014. A grand jury subsequently decided not to indict Wilson for Michael Brown's death.

3. A series of brunch interruptions staged by activists during 2015, emphasizing that while black lives are being lost to police brutality, there are no peaceful spaces.

THE RED AND THE BLACK

1. No relation.

2. The economics of labor-managed firms is a huge topic that raises a host of complex institutional questions lying beyond the scope of this chapter. (See Gregory Dow's *Governing the Firm* for a comprehensive treatment.) But as a matter of politics, the important thing to note is that with such firms there is no longer a systemic conflict between an autonomous capitalist or managerial class and the mass of the population. Of course, there are still clashing sectoral interests. But those exist no matter what property form is in place. Moreover, I think there is good reason to believe that the sway of parochial sectoral interests on politics is greater when

there is an autonomous capitalist class than when there is none, because that class has an intrinsic interest in maintaining the porousness of the state to self-seeking minority interests *in general*.

3. There's no need to assume that managers must necessarily collect pecuniary rewards for better performance. But using that assumption makes possible a simple mathematical illustration of how managers can be evaluated on relative but not absolute profits. Suppose that at the start of each year the authorities decided on a certain fraction of national income that would be devoted to paying managerial bonuses at the end of the year. The number could change each year, but let's say this year it's 3 percent. When the year is out, national income is added up, along with total profit. If total profit comes to 30 percent of national income, that means total bonuses will be a tenth of total profits (3 percent divided by 30 percent), which means the bonus pool for *each firm's* managers will be equal to a tenth of *that firm's* profits. Under a system like this, each manager would have an interest in improving her *own* firm's profit performance; but she would have no rational reason to subvert or object to any general profit-suppressing laws, norms, customs, or regulations enacted in the public interest, assuming they applied to all firms equally. Again, what's important here is the concept: whether it's money or praise that is awarded for good performance, the principle is the same.

CONTRIBUTORS

Seth Ackerman is on the editorial board of *Jacobin* and a doctoral candidate in history at Cornell University.

Phillip Agnew is the executive director and cofounder of the Dream Defenders, a community activist group of minority youth who have been recognized as the next generation of civil rights leaders.

Tim Barker graduated from Columbia University in 2013. His work has appeared in *N +1*, *Dissent*, the *Nation*, and the *New Inquiry*.

Dante Barry is the executive director of the Million Hoodies Movement for Justice.

Alyssa Battistoni is on the editorial board of *Jacobin*. Her writing has been published in *Salon*, *Mother Jones*, and *Alternet*. She lives in New Haven, Connecticut.

Cherrell Carruthers is a national organizer for Equal Justice USA.

Megan Erickson is on the editorial board of *Jacobin*, and is the author of *Class War: The Privatization of Childhood*. She has worked as a teacher and administrator in public and private schools throughout New York City. She currently oversees preschool, afterschool, and summer camp programs at the YMCA.

Peter Frase is a PhD student in sociology at the CUNY Graduate Center in New York. He is also an editor at *Jacobin* and the author of *Four Futures*.

Llewellyn Hinkes-Jones writes on science and technology and has published in the *Atlantic*, the *New York Times*, *The Awl*, *Jacobin*, and the *Los Angeles Review of Books*.

Sarah Leonard is senior editor at the *Nation*, editor-at-large at *Dissent* and a contributing editor at the *New Inquiry*. She also teaches at New York University's Gallatin School. She lives in New York City.

Chris Maisano is a writer and activist based in Brooklyn. He is a union researcher and a contributing editor at *Jacobin*.

Jesse A. Myerson, an activist who lives in New York City, has written for *Rolling Stone* magazine and the *Nation*.

Kate Redburn is a JD-PhD student at Yale Law School and the Yale Department of History. She has worked as a community organizer in New York and as a photographer and oral historian in Argentina thanks to a Fulbright research grant. A contributing editor at *Jacobin*, her work has also appeared in *Salon*, *Dissent*, and the *New Inquiry*.

Mychal Denzel Smith is a Knobler Fellow at The Nation Institute.

Tony Smith is a professor of philosophy at Iowa State University and the author of *Technology and Capital in the Age of Lean Production*.

Bhaskar Sunkara is the founding editor and publisher of *Jacobin*.

Ashley Yates is an activist, poet, and artist raised in Florissant, Missouri, who is also cocreator of Millennial Activist United.